CW00555615

Seafarer & Community

Seafarer & Community

TOWARDS A SOCIAL UNDERSTANDING OF SEAFARING

EDITED BY PETER H. FRICKE

CROOM HELM LONDON

ROWMAN & LITTLEFIELD, NEW JERSEY

First published 1973
© 1973 by Croom Helm Ltd

Croom Helm Ltd
2–10 St Johns Road London SW 11

ISBN 0–85664–041–7

This book is distributed in the United States of America
by Rowman & Littlefield, Publishers
The Library Division of Littlefield, Adams & Company
81 Adams Drive, Totowa, New Jersey, 07512

Printed in Great Britain by Richard Clay (*The Chaucer Press*), *Ltd.*,
Bungay, Suffolk

For BETTY,
who helped and encouraged.

Contents

List of figures and tables

Preface

Most of the papers appearing in this book were prepared for a 'Symposium on Seafarer and Community' held at the University of Wales Institute of Science and Technology in May, 1972. Since then they have been revised and developed into their present form, as a move towards an interdisciplinary understanding of the life of the seafarer.

Obviously the choice of papers for a symposium or a book of this kind is selective and reflects the organiser or editor's own interests. It is believed that others will be interested and stimulated too. Academic knowledge advances through argument and discussion, and the contributors and editor hope that this will take place.

As editor, one must acknowledge the help and effort given by all concerned. To my fellow contributors I owe a debt of gratitude for their hard work in preparing their papers. To Christopher Helm I am similarly indebted for his advice and patience during the lengthy process of turning papers into a book. Jennifer Hurn and Jean Watkins typed and retyped drafts cheerfully and frequently under the pressure of time. Finally, I must accept any errors of translation, interpretation or omission as my responsibility, and hope that the reader will find this collection of articles of interest.

Cardiff   PETER H. FRICKE
July, 1973

Notes on the Contributors

Raoul Andersen is Associate Professor in the Department of Sociology and Anthropology, Memorial University of Newfoundland. His research interests lie in the study of fishing communities, and he has published extensively in this field.

Michael S. Bassis is Instructor in Sociology at the University of Rhode Island. His research interests are in the field of the Sociology of Education, particularly the socialisation and organisational aspects of higher education.

Bernardo Cattarinussi is an Associate of the Institute of International Sociology, Gorizia, Italy. He has specialised in the study of communities in the Gorizia, and has undertaken research in fishing villages on the West coast of Italy.

Peter H. Fricke is Lecturer in Ship Management and Maritime Sociology in the Department of Maritime Studies, University of Wales Institute of Science and Technology. His research interests are the study of seafaring communities and ships' crews from an organisational and industrial perspective. He was formerly a seafarer.

Warren H. Hopwood is Senior Lecturer in the School of Maritime Studies, College of Further Education, Plymouth. He is concerned with the training of seafarers, and has conducted extensive research into maritime education. Captain Hopwood served in the Merchant Navy.

Jan Horbulewicz is Director of the Central Laboratory of Marine Psychology and Sociology, Gdynia, Poland. A psychologist, he has conducted a great deal of research into the human aspects of fishing and life at sea.

Bryan Nolan is Lecturer in Sociology in the Department of Humanities and Social Studies at the Polytechnic of the South Bank, London. A former seafarer, he is concerned with studies of socialisation to the occupation.

William R. Rosengren is Professor of Sociology at the University of Rhode Island. His research interests are in the fields of complex organisations and social organisation. He has published extensively.

Hance D. Smith is Lecturer in Human Geography at the Aberdeen College of Education. A Shetlander, he has a continuing research interest in the economic and human geography of fisheries and remote communities.

R. Geoffrey Stiles is Assistant Professor in the Department of Sociology and Anthropology at Memorial University of Newfoundland. He is presently engaged in research into the structural and organisational aspects of maritime communities.

One · Seafarer and Community

PETER H. FRICKE

INTRODUCTION

The life of the seafarer has attracted the attention of non-seafarers through the ages. The romanticists and modern cruise publicists dwell on the exotic places and personages which can only be seen by going to sea. The bravery and adventures of seafarers are also sung by popular poets and writers. The purpose of this book is to attempt to view the life of the seafarer from another perspective: a form of occupational community. The eyes that we use are those of anthropologists and of economists; of geographers, psychologists, seafarers and sociologists. Our views differ in detail too, but the theme we have explored is the impact of technological and social change upon an occupational community. It is by the nature of seafaring that our perspective is international, for frequently the British A.B., the Canadian deckhand and the Italian fisherman share more cultural and social attributes in common than they share with non-seafarers of their respective countries. It is this phenomenon we will explore.

The Concept of Community

A seafarer rarely lives and works alone: the trans-Atlantic yachtsman is the epitome of an extreme type of leisure consumer; the seafarer, whether fisherman or merchant seaman, is at sea for economic reasons. His livelihood depends upon his success in his occupation. He works and lives with others because this reduces the level of risk inherent in working alone, and adds to the capital available for the exploitation of new technologies or markets, or the encouragement of existing skills. The relationships derived from working and living with others, from engaging in interdependent activities, are social relationships, and form the basis for the development of an occupational community.[1]

It is necessary to emphasise that these relationships are the prior condition of an occupational community, but they do not imply that a true community is present. MacIver recognised this in his definition of community:

A community is a focus of social life, the common living of social beings; an association is an organization of social life, definitely established for the pursuit of one or more common interests. An association is partial, a community is integral . . . Within a community there may exist not only numerous associations but also antagonistic associations.[2]

As communities have developed over the ages, they have increased in both size and technological complexity. The division of labour has become increasingly marked, and while the Malay, Newfoundland and Italian fishing villages studied by social anthropologists exhibit the characteristics of an occupational community, the fishermen of Hull and Gdynia form an occupational sub-group within a much larger community.[3] Merchant seamen also follow this trend in the dilution of occupational communities as the proportion of seafarers has declined in relation to the numbers of persons engaged in other occupational groups in traditional seaport communities. In the United Kingdom this communal dilution has been accompanied by an absolute decline in the numbers of merchant seamen. In 1948 approximately 200,000 men were serving on board British ships, while in 1967 approximately 127,500 men earned their living on merchant ships.[4]

Thus, the concept of community is relative to the perspective of the researcher and his subjects. The ambience of a community, the reality of its existence, may still be seen by its inhabitants as due to a particular occupational activity. We are told by Tunstall that fishing employs, directly or indirectly, only $6\frac{1}{2}$ per cent of all employed persons in Hull.[5] Hull has a very large deep-sea trawler fleet, but the 'community' of the modern fisherman is being dispersed to council housing estates on the outskirts of the city, while the traditional fishing quarter of Hessle Road is redeveloped as an industrial area thus increasing an already high dilution. In a study by D. Gaye Newton of fishing families in Milford Haven, west Wales, a similar pattern of dispersion was discovered. This dilution of the close-knit, seafaring-reliant community ashore has affected the attitudes of seafarers to their occupation. They have become involved to a greater extent in industrial organisations and systems, and the special ambience of community has vanished with the increasing division of labour and occupational opportunities of their society as a whole. Where the isolated community remains, so do many of the traditional values of fishing and seafarers.

Social scientists have concerned themselves largely with structural or systemic models of the societies and communities they have studied. But society is constantly changing, and the models derived of any one social situation become obsolete. Durkheim discussed this phenomena,[6] and noted that with the change in density of communities came a diminishing of some of the activities of the individual, but an increase in the possibilities for intellectual and occupational stimulation. The pattern of recruitment to occupations has changed in Britain since the 1944 Education Act guaranteed free secondary education for all. In shipping the economies of bulk-buying and use of shore facilities for repairs have eroded many of the traditional skills of the seafarer, and splicing, for example, is rarely performed on ship nowadays. With the use of nylon nets the skills of the 'twine maker' are also diminishing. The decline of skills, the places they held in ecomonic and status systems, and the advent of new skills effectively reduce the utility of social science models in the short term. The models, however, are important in the long term in that they permit a comparative study of the evolution of societies, and it is in this sense that we use the term community in this book. We conceive of a community as changing over time, of becoming differentiated with the advent of new skills, but also integrating itself through a common tradition and social life.

Seafaring as a Career

Seafaring has always concerned itself with its past:

> The present structure of command and of relationships aboard ship has grown up over a long period of time and has inevitably been influenced by past needs, some of which may not be so relevant today. Traditions are valuable in creating a pride of service, but they can become obstacles to further progress if they are allowed to go so far as to obscure the basic need for providing a competitive commercial organization.[7]

It is the past practices which, as in other occupations, provide a focus for present methods of organisation and a pattern of life for a member of the occupation. This pattern places the worker within the context of his workgroup; it determines his social status and forms of social activity, and his attitudes towards, and expectations of, society in general and his community in particular. Where occupation and community values are not in step, there will be pressures on the individual to renounce one or the other. As we will see, community values and seafaring values are similar in the small community, but diverge considerably in the larger forms of social organisation.

Men go to sea because of the rewards they receive for doing so. In a subsistence economy, fishing may be the only access to a reliable food resource for a family, community or society. In a highly developed industrial economy fishing becomes one of many ways in which a living can be earned, and the demand for fish reflects the availability of other food resources for purchase. The same pattern holds for the merchant seaman. Where the demand for his services are high, and so are his rewards, the merchant seaman will make seafaring his career. When the rewards are not adequate, a high rate of labour turnover will be evident in the occupation. Consequently the stability of occupational, and therefore communal, patterns of behaviour depend upon the perceived rewards of entering and remaining in the occupation. Rewards need not be economic in nature, and Moreby has noted that the relative deprivation of the home life of Merchant Navy recruits from Southern Ireland and the Shetlands may be a decisive factor in the high proportion making the sea their career.[8] In all cases men rarely stay at sea when other shore-based methods of obtaining economic rewards are available.[9]

Seafaring follows a cyclical pattern of early entry and early withdrawal in the employment chain. This is partly due to the heavy nature of the work on ships and fishing craft, to the changing status of older men within the community and to the requirements of the fishing and trade patterns. Smith and Cattarinussi discuss the effects of seasonal and lunar fluctuations in fishing patterns which afford the opportunities for fishermen to undertake other tasks ashore, or for leisure activities. Merchant seamen follow a cyclical pattern also, but it is more clearly marked among younger men on the North Atlantic trades. Here the seafarer will maximise his earnings during the summer and early autumn on the cargo-lines to North America, if he can obtain a berth. In the late autumn the seafarer will decide if he wishes to be home for Christmas, and if so, seeks a short voyage. The alternative taken by many of the seafarers is to obtain a ship to the Far East or Australasia during the period of the worst weather in the Atlantic and return to Europe in the late spring. This working of voyages allows for variety, but also places the less able or older man in the difficult position of only obtaining berths during the worst (and most physically demanding) weather or on irregular runs on which the economic rewards are not great.

The ship or fishing vessel does provide a rhythmic or cyclical pattern in the life of the community. Its sailings and arrivals, the pattern of work to be done, and the organisation of the crew form the basic for the social structure of the ship-as-community and for the social system ashore. As the technology becomes more sophisticated and an increasing division of labour evolves so too does a status system which is unrelated to the ascribed statuses of kinship, sex and age. The development of the technologies of the sea have a profound effect on the ship's crew. The *Daghestan*, a modern bulk carrier of 25,000 deadweight tons with all crew accommodation on the after part of the vessel, has living quarters stratified by rank or achieved status. The largest cabin on the upper deck is for the ship's master. On the deck below, in smaller cabins, are the majority of the ship's officers, and ten men are accommodated on this deck. On the main deck the sailors, engine-room hands and stewards have their small cabins, and nineteen men share this area. For carpeting, a recognised status symbol, the master's cabin has wall-to-wall carpets, the officers' cabins have throw-rugs and the ratings' cabins have linoleum. The effect of these divisions on the basis of 'achieved status' is to create economic and social cleavages in the community ashore.

This identification of, and with, occupational statuses is the key to an understanding of the effects of technological change on seafarers and their communal life. The division of labour at sea has effectively changed the density of communal links because few homogeneous groups are involved in the seafaring occupations which are large enough to retain an identity within the context of shore society. The description 'seafarer' in this sense is a misnomer as it masks varied skills and status levels.

A further consequence of the dilution of occupational community and the division of labour on board ship is a lack of shared experience and hence the reinforcement of communal identification. The life and work of a seagoing electrician is very different from that of a deck hand or steward. The difference in experience of life at sea is frequently so great that no cohesion of the crew as an occupational group occurs. A frequent statement encountered by researchers on merchant vessels and fishing craft is, 'I have no friends at sea; only Board of Trade acquaintances.' The lack of affective ties is a function of the division of labour, lack of communal support and the frequency with which crews change their membership. As we will see later, there is a striking continuity in the membership of crews with a communal base in merchant ships. This continuity is partly the result of the seafarer's weighing factors, such as company, master or skipper, length of run, or time of year, but in all cases crews recruited from one locale stay together for a longer period of time than crews recruited from a wider region.

The papers included in this book were prepared for, or developed from, papers presented at the symposium 'Seafarer and Community' held in 1972 by the Department of Maritime Studies, University of Wales Institute of Science and Technology. The format is dictated by the development of two major themes at the symposium. The first theme is change and its consequences in fishing communities. The papers develop the twin themes of historical economic development and technological change in fishing and its social environment. The contributions are introduced by Hance Smith's study of the Shetland fisheries, and explored by Bernardo Cattarinussi's description of technological change in the fisheries in the Upper Adriatic Sea, and by Raoul Andersen and Geoffrey Stiles' study of Newfoundland fishermen. Jan Horbulewicz takes the theme up in his exploration of the psychic demands imposed on modern industrial fishermen by their occupation, and Bryan Nolan discusses the concept of the total institution as it would appear to apply to the ship-as-community.

The problems of socialisation and acculturalisation to an occupation are then discussed by Warren Hopwood in his study of the training of Merchant Navy cadet officers, and by Michael Bassis and William Rosengren in their research into the development of maritime training in Britain, Spain and the United States. The final paper attempts to synthesise these problems and relate them to a study of families of the crews of British merchant ships.

REFERENCES

1. R. M. MacIver, *Community*, Macmillan, London, 1924, p. 6.
2. Ibid., p. 24.
3. See, for example, R. Andersen and C. Wadel, (eds.), *North Atlantic Fishermen*, Memorial University Press, Newfoundland, 1972; T. M. Fraser, *Rusembilan*, Cornell University Press, 1960,

Ithaca, N.Y.; B. Cattarinussi, in this book; G. W. Horobin, 'Community & Occupation in the Hull Fishing Industry', in *British Journal of Sociology*, Vol. VIII, no. 4, 1957, pp. 343–56; and J. Horbulewicz, in this book.

4. J. M. M. Hill, *The Seafaring Career*, Tavistock, London, Institute of Human Relations, 1972, p. 7.

5. J. Tunstall, *The Fishermen*, McGibbon & Kee, London, 1962, pp. 77–8.

6. E. Durkheim, *Division of Labour in Society* (trans. G. Simpson), Free Press, Glencoe, Ill., 1947, p. 347.

7. Rochdale Committee, paragraph 17.

8. D. H. Moreby, *Personnel Management in Merchant Ships*, London, Pergamon, 1969.

9. See, for example, T. Hogg, 'Man in the Marine Environment', UWIST, Cardiff, Unpublished seminar paper, 1971; T. M. Fraser, op. cit.

Two · The Development of Shetland Fisheries and Fishing Communities

HANCE D. SMITH

This paper analyses the geographical factors that shape the development of fisheries and fishing communities in the Shetland Islands. Shetland is one of a large number of so-called 'traditional' fishing areas, associated with fisheries over centuries. These regions are common along stretches of coast on both sides of the North Atlantic; they exist in Newfoundland, around the coasts of the British Isles and in western Norway. The fishing communities in these areas tend to take the form of villages and small towns, or dispersed agricultural settlements based on small-holdings. The geographical background is of particular importance, as they have generally been influenced by environmental factors in their early stages, when the technology of fishing was relatively primitive. Thus their evolution is inseparable from that of the fisheries with which they were originally associated. While the starting point for discussion of Shetland fisheries and fishing communities centres round their environmental setting, the starting point for the analysis of the geographical factors involved is the history of the development of the fisheries.

The first phase in the evolution of the present Shetland communities can be traced vaguely to the pre-eighteenth century fisheries. It was followed by the development of the open-boat 'haaf' * fishery until the early nineteenth century. Third was the cod fishery, the rise of which took place in two stages, from 1815 until 1830, and again from 1855 until 1870. Partly overlapping this phase was the herring fishery using half-decked boats,* which lasted from 1825 until the early 1840s. The final phase was the complex sequence of events leading to the decline and disappearance of the haaf and cod fisheries, and the rise of the herring, spring-line and haddock fisheries in the period between 1880 and 1914. By the outbreak of the First World War, the present pattern of fishing communities had become established. The historical development of Shetland fishing communi-

---

* Terms shown thus are defined in the Glossary on page 28.

8

ties points to a number of geographical factors, which can be further clarified by comparisons with certain other important fishing areas in north-west Europe.

There are two basic, unchanging environmental factors which have shaped the geography of fishing in the Shetland area. The first of these is the location of the archipelago near the centre of that portion of the continental shelf to the north of the British Isles, and to the west of the Norwegian Deep (Fig. 2.1). The northern part of the North Sea is the most important fishing region in the whole of the north-west European shelf sea area which has meant that at various times in the past the islands have been used as a base for large-scale herring fishing, long-line fishing for ling and hand-line fishing for cod by vessels from outwith the islands, even so this foreign fishing activity has had limited influence on the growth of local fisheries and fishing communities. The most important influence has been the second factor, local environmental characteristics.

At the local scale, the islands have been noted throughout history for their locally based fisheries. This has been expressed in the recognition of the sea as 'the Shetlander's home and provider', by Russell, an outsider writing in 1897.[1] While it is the case that, in most periods in history, the fisheries have been the principal element in the trading economy, agriculture was also of importance as the subsistence counterpart to that economy until the beginning of the present century. This situation is summed up in the local nineteenth-century image of Shetland as the 'Aald (i.e. 'Old') Rock', an appellation which represented a strong identification of the islanders with their insular environment, stemming in part from the close-knit social and economic structure which characterised Shetland at that time, in which the resources of both land and sea played considerable parts in the economy.[2] Again, in the period since the Second World War, for example, it is only comparatively recently that the value of fisheries exports derived from locally owned production has substantially exceeded the value of the livestock and knitwear exports which are the other main export trade commodities.[3]

This balance in the use of land and sea resources has underlain the development of the fisheries and fishing communities throughout. While the term 'fishing community' infers a group of people depending primarily upon the fisheries as a means of earning a livelihood, the subsistence agricultural basis was a considerable component in the economy in the Shetlands. The basis of Shetland society was a class of farmer-fishermen, who lived to an appreciable extent off the

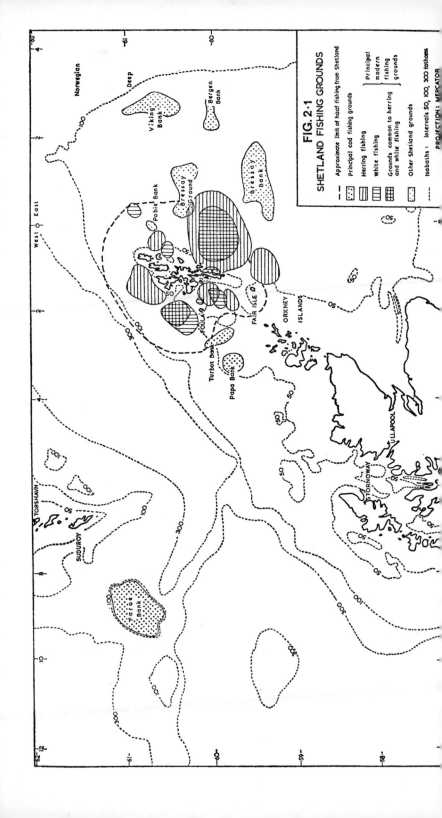

FIG. 2·1
SHETLAND FISHING GROUNDS

– – –	Approximate limit of haaf fishing from Shetland
⣿⣿	Principal cod fishing grounds
▥	Herring fishing
▤	White fishing
▦	Grounds common to herring and white fishing
⣿	Other Shetland grounds

Principal modern fishing grounds

isobaths : intervals 50, 100, 300 fathoms

PROJECTION : MERCATOR

Norwegian Deep

Viking Bank

Bergen Bank

Pobie Bank

Bressay Ground

Bressay Bank

West O East

FOULA

Papa Bank

Turbot Bank

FAIR ISLE

ORKNEY ISLANDS

ULLAPOOL

STORNOWAY

TORSHAVN

SUDUROY

Faroe Bank

land. Fishing communities did not begin to take shape until the changes which took place in the fisheries in the closing decades of the nineteenth century.

The influence of the physical environment was perhaps most profound during the first phase in the development of the fisheries. Before the beginning of the eighteenth century, the island economy[4] was based to a large degree on subsistence, with a concomitant dispersed agricultural settlement pattern, and nearshore subsistence fishing from open boats. There were no fishing communities as such, but a series of agricultural townships, each of which possessed boats, participating in both subsistence and commercial fishing. Apart from the sale of woollen stockings to the Dutch herring fishermen, who carried on their great summer herring fishing off the coasts throughout the seventeenth century, the commercial sector of the economy was based on the sale of butter and fish oil, paid as rent in kind, and on long-line fishing for ling, and to a lesser extent cod, from which derived the export of dry salt fish. This long-line fishery was the most important element in the export trade, controlled by German merchants from Hamburg and Bremen, who resorted annually to recognised trading points in order to make up their cargoes. They brought in meal, fishing materials and other goods which were often bartered for the fish.

The location of the merchants' booths,* together with scattered literature and documentary references, are the only indications of the geographical patterns of fishing at this period. This evidence is strongly suggestive of a pattern of small-scale inshore fishing, probably within ten miles of the shore, all round the coast and closely related to the settlement pattern, itself determined by subsistence agricultural requirements. After the prevention of the German merchants' trade by the Union of Scotland and England in 1707, and several unsuccessful attempts by Scottish and English merchants to take their place,[5] the burden of economic development fell upon the local landowners. In a subsistence society in which the land was capable of producing about eight months' supply of the staple oatmeal and beremeal in good years, the only practical possibility was the development of the fisheries, with agriculture maintaining its subsistence role in the economy. This took the form of the expansion and improvement of the open boat fishery, which became known as the haaf* fishery.

The expansion of the haaf fishing was associated with changes in fishing technology, and in the distribution of fishing activity. The boats used were of two types, the fourern* and sixern,* which had four and six oars respectively. The smaller fourern was normally used in nearshore fishing, while the larger sixern was used mainly in offshore fishing. The method of fishing[6] was by means of long-line, which consisted of a series of separate lines of 'baukts'.* On each baukt, which was 40 to 50 fathoms long, hooks were spaced at regular intervals of $3\frac{1}{2}$ to 5 fathoms, attached by means of snoods or 'toms'* 3 to 4 feet long. The baukts were tied together as the lines were laid, the numbers of baukts per boat varying from as low as 30 to 40 to a maximum of around 120, depending on whether she was engaged in nearshore or offshore fishing.

The locational pattern of production tended to be governed in the first instance by the location of the resource base. Throughout the period, ling was the staple export, and ling was most abundant on the wide, even expanses of the continental shelf, generally farthest from land. Consequently, the most important haaf fishing areas tended to be situated round the periphery of the archipelago (Fig. 2.2A), particularly the 'far haaf' stations used by boats fishing at the extreme limits of haaf fishing (Fig. 2.1). A further advantage was that the peripheral areas closest to the fishing grounds, with their pre-dominantly igneous and sandstone rocks and their large expanses of exposed and semi-exposed coastline, usually have the greatest number of stony beaches suitable for curing and drying, and many of these beaches became established stations. Stations from which the nearshore fishery using fourerns was prosecuted can be distinguished from those concerned with the offshore fishery by studying the aver-age number of baukts carried by each boat. The number of baukts was roughly in direct proportion to the distance offshore, not least because the room available for laying lines also increased in direct proportion to the distance from shore.[7]

The most fundamental division which appeared was between peripheral and central areas (Fig. 2.2A), the former tending to specialise in offshore 'far haaf' fisheries for ling off the eastern, northern and north-western shores; and the latter almost exclusively in nearshore fisheries. In the peripheral area, where the sea area was most extensive, the number of lines carried by each boat was greatest. The fishing methods of the Northmavine area are the outstanding example of this. In outlying areas where there were shallows and strong tidal conditions, inshore fisheries tended to be dominant, with relatively small numbers of baukts per boat, the most important of these districts being Dunrossness, where the saithe fishery was of

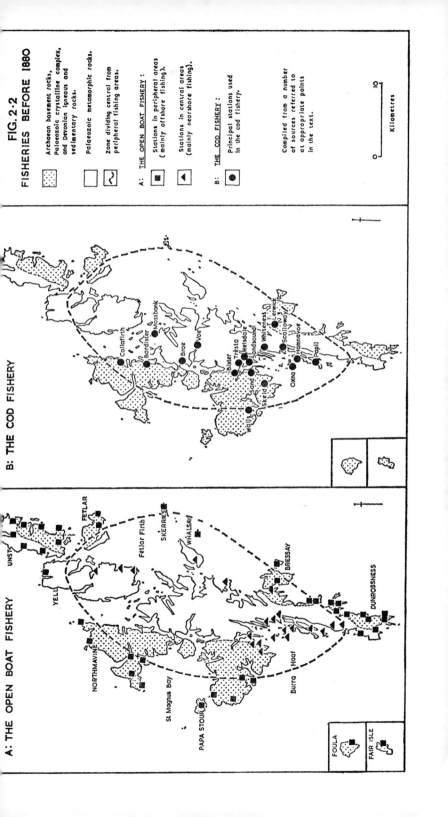

FIG. 2.2
FISHERIES BEFORE 1880

Archaean basement rocks, Palaeozoic crystalline complex, and Devonian igneous and sedimentary rocks.

Palaeozoic metamorphic rocks.

Zone dividing central from peripheral fishing areas.

A: THE OPEN BOAT FISHERY:

Stations in peripheral areas (mainly offshore fishing).

Stations in central areas (mainly nearshore fishing).

B: THE COD FISHERY:

Principal stations used in the cod fishery.

Compiled from a number of sources referred to at appropriate points in the text.

0   10
Kilometres

B: THE COD FISHERY

Collafirth
Mossbank
Bardister
Voe
Brae
Bixter
Tresta
Whiteness
Lerwick
Wellsdale
Sandsound
Scalloway
Hamnavoe
Oxna
Papil
Scousburgh
Skeld
Wull

FOULA
FAIR ISLE

A: THE OPEN BOAT FISHERY

UNST
YELL
FETLAR
Fetlar Firth
SKERRIES
WHALSAY
NORTHMAVINE
St Magnus Bay
BRESSAY
PAPA STOUR
Burra Haaf
DUNROSSNESS
FOULA
FAIR ISLE

greatest importance; Foula, which specialised in cod fishing to some extent,[8] and Fair Usle. Unst was to a small extent a saithe fishery centre,[9] while Skerries was in a favourable location for both inshore and offshore fishing.

The central nearshore waters consisted of five areas.[10] Undoubtedly, the most important of these was the Burra Haaf, in which cod fishing was probably marginally of greater importance than ling, and fishing was carried on commercially in winter as well as in summer. The proximity of the grounds was a decisive advantage in this respect. The second most important area was the deep basin south of Fetlar known today as the Fetlar Firth or Bight, used by boats from Whalsay, Skerries and south and east Yell; Yell Sound was the leading piltock * fishing area; St. Magnus Bay and the area north of Bressay were much less important. Along the west coast of Mainland, herring were sometimes caught in the voes * in the harvest months, but this was an intermittent and unimportant fishery in the export trade as a whole.

There are two strong lines of evidence which illustrate the increasing importance of offshore fishery development in the peripheral areas in the course of the eighteenth century, and demonstrate the relationship between the haaf fishery and social development. The first of these was the seasonal migration of labour to the fishing stations from the central region,[11] which was very marked, particularly in the latter half of the century. The concentration of the major expansion into the second part of the century is also often hinted at by references to the earlier greater importance of farming, especially stock rearing, in some of the central parishes. This migration of labour was paralleled, as the population increased, by growth in the number of agricultural holdings, mainly in the peripheral areas. These additional holdings were able to accommodate a greater number of subsistence tenant-fishermen, and were created by the subdivision of existing holdings, and the creation of new arable enclosures known as 'outsets'.

The new holdings were perhaps the most tangible evidence of that second indicator of expansion, the landowners' interest in acquiring land in suitable fishing localities, evidenced early in the century by competition for favourable peripheral locations.[12] There was a tendency, for example, for those more powerful landowners whose estates were centred in areas remote from the periphery to acquire land interests in the outer region, and by the end of the century the periphery was characterised by the presence of relatively large estates belonging to landowners primarily engaged in the haaf fishing. The pressure of landowning interests tending towards the periphery resulted in land values rising in these areas, irrespective of the quality of the land for agriculture, such land selling for 50 to 70 and even 100 times the annual rental value in the 1780s. In contrast, land in areas remote from offshore fishery development remained relatively stable in price.

On the whole, it is notable that fishing communities did not appear at this time. Social adjustment took the form of migration of labour and the growth of large estates. Although the basic reasons for this were economic, a strong social cohesion in the islands was also apparent, caused by the advent of fishing tenures, whereby the tenants were bound to the several landowners, their security of tenure being dependent upon their fishing for them in return for supplies of fishing materials and meal to cover the shortfall in subsistence agricultural production. However, the fishing tenure system did not come into being immediately.[13] In the first half of the eighteenth century it is likely that the landowner–tenant relationship was a relatively free one in an economic sense. The landowner bought the tenant's fish in return for the supply of fishing materials. None the less, the landowner was also a landowner *per se*, accepting payment in kind (butter and fish oil) of his rent from the tenant-fisherman.

In theory, there is no reason why these two sides of the landowner's business should not have remained distinct. In practice, there were three main reasons which made the independence of landowning on the one hand, and participation in the fish trade on the other, at best precarious, and at worst inseparable. Perhaps the most important of these was the seasonal nature of agricultural and fishery production, a direct consequence of climate and hydrographic factors, which caused a summer peak in business. This, coupled with the basic inadequacy of agricultural production, necessitated the advancement of credit to the tenant, usually in the form of meal and fishing materials.

A second drawback was that the products used in rent payment, especially the butter and oil, remained for a long time of poor quality, and fetched low prices at market. As quality and prices improved, there arose a situation in which, when prices were high, the tenants tended to sell their butter to the merchants, while conversely, the tenants would pay it to the landowner when market prices were low.[14] Further, the pressure on the tenants to pay in kind if prices were high was great, and might well be beyond their ability,[15] thus rendering unavoidable rent payment in the chief trade commodity, fish.[16]

These problems of seasonality of credit and blurring of the distinction between rent and trade commodities might have been ameliorated had there been an adequate money supply to iron out the fluctuations in liquidity to which the tenants were subject. However, the surplus of credit acquired in good years was not reflected in money savings. The money supply was generally inadequate, and consisted mainly of debased German and Dutch coinage, which could be exchanged for British money only in Orkney,[17] whence came meal supplies.

The cumulative effect of these three factors was that, by the 1770s and 1780s, a significant proportion of the rent was from time to time being paid in fish. Indeed, in the peripheral haaf areas favourable for fishing, the rents were often artificially low and compensated for by the profits of the fisheries, while landowners in the central region tended to make their tenants pay higher rents and sell their fish below the current market price.[18] Little could be done about the physical and economic insecurity apart from the time-honoured social adjustments of short leases for the tenants (which were, in effect, no leases at all), and short tacks * for the tacksmen,* who sometimes leased the landowners' properties, usually to engage in the fish trade. As the haaf fishing developed, it gradually became understood that the fisherman was to sell his fish to the landowner in return for security of tenure on his land—in short, this was the system of fishing tenures, which secured, as far as possible, the incomes of both. Growing out of necessity in the first part of the eighteenth century, it was becoming a burden for both landowners and tenants by the end of the century.

The fishing tenure system could not really be altered until the rise of merchants as middlemen made it possible to separate the business of landowning and rent collection in organisational terms from that of fishing and trading. Even then, in the period 1790 until 1820, the first generation of merchants were usually landowners as well, and it was only in the period 1820 until 1840 that the fishing tenure system passed away to a considerable extent under the influence of increasing prosperity and the rise of a class of small shopkeepers.[19] This increase in prosperity, associated with the passing of initiative in trade and economic development from landowners to merchants, was in no small measure due to the interests of the merchants in developing the cod and herring fisheries after the Napoleonic Wars. The haaf fishing stopped expanding in the 1780s, and remained static until the 1810s, after which it tended to expand further in parallel with the rise of the cod fishing.

The growth of the locational pattern of the cod fishing from around 1815 onwards was closely governed by two factors, the location of the cod fishing grounds in relation to the islands as a whole, and the contrasting patterns of landholding interests between the central and peripheral regions of activity which had developed in the haaf era. To begin with, the cod fishing grounds were situated almost entirely to the west and south-west of the archipelago, in areas such as the Turbot and Papa Banks (Fig. 2.1), and were exploited using fully decked sloops and hand lines. The use of these large decked vessels, with their greater speed and ability to stay at sea in conditions which would have forced the open boats ashore, changed the situation where the western side of the islands was more valuable than the eastern because it was closer to the cod grounds. However, the cod fishery did not take root in the peripheral area on the West Side. The decisive factors in location were the physical suitability of the central region, and the pattern of landholding.[20]

The central region (Fig. 2.2B) could provide the harbour facilities necessary for large vessels, whereas the peripheral area could not. Here, the characteristic alternating ridge and valley topography intersects the coast to produce the long, narrow and comparatively sheltered voe, with small offshore islands. The floors of the voes generally consist of sand and mud, which is good anchorage ground. It was this combination of room, anchorage ground and shelter which was the important physical factor in the determination of the location of shore stations.[21]

The other decisive factor was the pattern of landholding. By this time the peripheral areas tended to consist of relatively few large estates dominated by the haaf-fishing landowners, while the central area consisted of a greater number of smaller estates, some of whose landlords entered business as merchants, and pioneered investment in the cod fishing. The continuing system of fishing tenures in the haaf fishing areas, and the rise in population, provided a stable background which tended to favour the expansion of both types of fishing and their continuing geographical separation. However, it did not favour the growth of fishing communities, as the cod fishermen also were tied to their subsistence holdings.

In the first phase of expansion of the home cod fishery, between

1815 and 1830, places round the West Side in the vicinity of Scalloway tended to predominate. During the second phase of expansion, between 1855 and 1870, when a larger class of cod smacks ranged as far as Faroe, Rockall and Iceland (Fig. 2.1), western and northern districts also came into prominence, including Voe, Brae Collafirth in Northmavine and Mossbank (Fig. 2.2B). Although the small-scale landowners, and merchants were the chief investors in this fishery, there was for the first time, especially in the 1820s, appreciable investment by fishermen owning shares in sloops, in Burra and Scalloway. Despite the fact that there is not much evidence bearing on the connection between sloop-owning areas and prosperity in the open-boat fishing, it is known that even as early as 1809 the Burra men were reputed to be rich, due to their ability to carry on fishing on grounds relatively near to the shore, and all year round,[22] which would have provided a satisfactory economic basis for investment in cod fishing. In the second phase of expansion, merchant family firms provided most of the capital, and the majority of these firms were situated on the West Side.

The growth of the herring fishing in the 1820s was, like the cod fishing, closely associated with mercantile enterprise.[23] Using half-decked boats of various descriptions, imported from the east coast of Scotland, the merchants built it up between 1825 and 1835. It collapsed between 1840 and 1842, although some herring fishing was done, using sixerns, after the haaf fishing season until the late 1860s. Where herring fishing was carried on in small sailboats, proximity to the fishing grounds was a particularly important factor as, unlike line fishing, a round trip had to be made daily in order to land the herring as fresh as possible, to allow curing to begin without delay. Although these boats could not be operated from open beaches (which were in any case unsuitable for herring curing purposes), harbour facilities were less important than for cod fishing. Thus the herring stations tended to be located in peripheral areas which provided some shelter. Unlike the later development of the herring fishery, after 1880, this fishery was confined mainly to the east side, fishing the North Sea stock of herring, after the cod and haaf seasons were over in August. The central-peripheral subdivision was much less prominent, and the availability of harbours favoured some central area locations, such as Lerwick and Burravoe, while a series of important stations were established in peripheral areas, as near as possible to the offshore grounds, notably at Skerries, Cullivoe in Yell, Uyeasound and Balta-sound in Unst and the Sandwick area in Dunrossness (Fig. 2.3A).

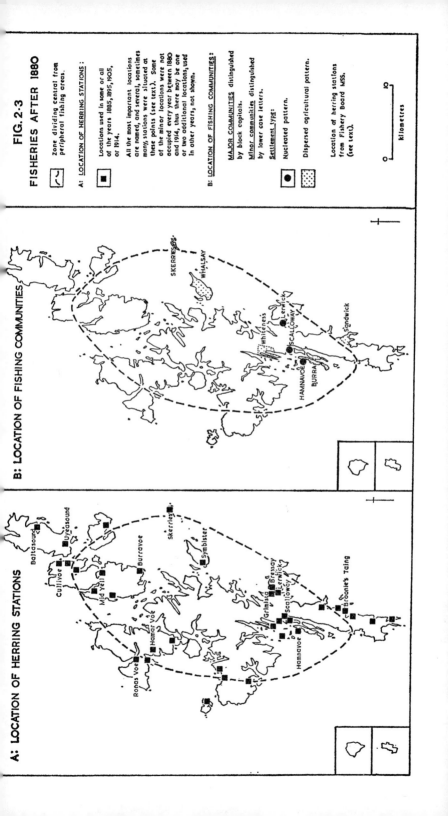

FIG. 2·3
FISHERIES AFTER 1880

Zone dividing central from peripheral fishing areas.

A: LOCATION OF HERRING STATIONS:

Locations used in some or all of the years 1885, 1895, 1905, or 1914.

All the most important locations are named, and several, sometimes many, stations were situated at these points (see text). Some of the minor locations were not occupied every year between 1880 and 1914, thus there may be one or two additional locations, used in other years, not shown.

B: LOCATION OF FISHING COMMUNITIES:

MAJOR COMMUNITIES distinguished by block capitals.
Minor communities distinguished by lower case letters.

Settlement type:
   ● Nucleated pattern.
   ▨ Dispersed agricultural pattern.

Location of herring stations from Fishery Board MSS. (see text).

0   10
kilometres

B: LOCATION OF FISHING COMMUNITIES

SKERRIES
WHALSAY
Whiteness
Lerwick
SCALLOWAY
HAMNAVOE
BURRA
Sandwick

A: LOCATION OF HERRING STATIONS

Baltasound
Uyeasound
Cullivoe
Mid Yell
Burravoe
Hamar Voe
Ronas Voe
Skerries
Symbister
Grimista
Bressay
Lerwick
Scalloway
Hamnavoe
Broonie's Taing

Because the herring fishing season did not interfere with haaf and cod fishing times, it was invested in by the haaf-fishing landowners, as well as by the cod merchants. However, as in the case of the haaf and cod fishings, this did not result in the formation of fishing communities; the subsistence agricultural pattern remained supreme. In order to understand how this occurred without the 'segregation' of separate fishing communities, it is necessary to examine in more detail the relationship between the fishermen on the one hand, and the merchants on the other.

The decline of the fishing tenure system between 1820 and 1840 did not overcome the problem of lack of credit due to seasonal factors and harvest and fishing failures. It was necessary for the new generation of merchants and shopkeepers to advance credit to the fishermen. Again, a largely unwritten understanding came into being, whereby the merchant ensured his income through the condition that the fisherman sold his fish to the merchant in return for supplies purchased (usually on credit) at the merchant's shop. Thus the fishing tenure system was supplanted by a truck system. There was a variety of arrangements in the various fisheries. In the haaf fishery, the large merchants gradually acquired estates, and in any case usually leased the fishings. Similar arrangements prevailed in the herring fishing. In the cod fishing, the vessels generally belonged to the merchants and were used also in trading. The agreements between owners and crews[24] usually stipulated that the catch was to be disposed of to the owner, although half of it commonly belonged to the owner in the first place, while the crew sold him their half.

From around the middle of the nineteenth century a number of factors contrived to break the long-standing links of fishing tenures and truck for goods. By the 1840s, although the largest merchants had become the largest landowners, landowning had become separately organised from fishing. The landowners were turning towards agricultural improvement, whereas merchants were concentrating on advancing the fisheries. Hence the basic insurance represented by fishing tenures was no longer required, and in the absence of legal security of tenure, which did not come until the Crofters' Holdings Act of 1886, landowners were more disposed towards evicting their tenants to promote agricultural improvements. On a substantial number of estates, where the landowner was also a merchant, this usually involved merely shifting the tenant to a poorer part of the estate in order to lay out farms on the better land, although a few landowners (usually with negligible fishing interests), evicted their tenants outright.[25] Meanwhile, the truck system gradually declined after the enquiries of the Truck Commission in 1871, and was replaced by systems of agreements between fishermen on the one hand and merchants and curers engaged in the fish trades on the other. In the case of the herring trade, the severe imbalances between supply and demand led to the introduction of an auction system in 1894 to replace the system of agreements between curers and fishermen.[26] The result of these developments was that the fishermen were freed of binding agreements with landowners, merchants or curers.

The phase from around 1870 until 1914 was characterised by three major developments: namely, the decline and eventual disappearance of the traditional haaf and cod fisheries; the rise of the herring, spring line and haddock fisheries; and a process of increasing specialisation in fisheries in various districts, accompanied by the establishment of the present-day geographical pattern of fishing communities.

Before 1870 there was a unity of land and sea in the economy, expressed in the division of labour of the crofter-fishermen between the two, in both central and peripheral regions. However, in the 1870s the traditional patterns of peripheral haaf fishing, dominated by merchants leasing fishing-grounds from landowners, and central merchant-dominated cod fishing, began to break up. The changing circumstances concerning land tenure and truck were undoubtedly partly responsible for this state of affairs. It was no longer necessary for the haaf fisherman in particular to remain burdened with debt to his landlord, while in the new economic conditions the opportunity to take up other forms of employment became much more realistic. Many emigrated, while several thousand took up employment in the merchant marine. The 1870s witnessed also the birth of a market-orientated, as distinct from a subsistence, economy.[27] It had become much more efficient to conduct one's material existence by concentrating entirely upon commercial production, and buying the necessities of life, including meal ground from cheap imported grain,[28] in return. Thus there was a tendency towards decline in subsistence agriculture.

These new market forces were undoubtedly partly responsible for the decline in the haaf fishing and cod fishing, the produce of which came into competition more and more with that of other areas. The cod fishing lost ground to developments in Faroe, where a large fleet of cod smacks was being built up, and Faroese dried fish were beginning to come into serious competition with the Shetland product in the main Spanish market,[29] to which the haaf fisheries' production was also directed. In the market economy the part-subsistence and part-commercial haaf production system, unchanged in essence from that of the eighteenth century, was in the weakest position economically, and without the shelter of truck tended to decline most rapidly. Under these circumstances, the fisheries gradually became localised in districts best suited to all-year-round fishing, while other areas were characterised by little or no fishing.

The development of the herring, spring line and haddock fishings proceeded from the late 1870s onwards. As in the previous phase of development of the herring fishing in the 1830s, herring stations (Fig. 2.3A) were not fishing communities. The type of vessel used was the fully decked lugger of 30 to 40 feet, and the fishermen lived aboard their boats during the herring season, travelling home at weekends. Unlike the earlier phase, however, the fishing was divided into early and late seasons. The early season, which lasted from May until the beginning of July, was concentrated on fishing the Atlanto-Scandinavian herring group on the west and north-west coasts of the archipelago, from stations on the West Side and in the North Isles (Fig. 2.3A). The late herring fishing began about the middle of July and lasted until the end of August or beginning of September. It was based on the North Sea herring stock.[30] Many of the herring stations on the West Side were vacated, and the fishing concentrated on the East Side grounds. This pattern was disrupted in 1905 when the West Side fishing failed. Although there was a partial recovery in fish stocks in later years the pattern was not resumed because the advent of the steam drifter made it possible to operate further afield, particularly from the West Side grounds (Fig. 2.1) to Lerwick.

The first phase of expansion of the herring fishery lasted from 1876 until 1885, and was characterised by the remarkably widespread acquisition of boats.[31] However, there were certain areas which tended to specialise in the herring fishery, mainly in the central zone, in districts which were also closest to the haddock fishing grounds, adjacent to the Burra Haaf and Fetlar Firth, and south of Lerwick. There were particular concentrations of boat ownership in Burra, Scalloway, Whiteness, Sandwick, Lerwick and Whalsay (Fig. 2.3B).

As in the days of the old inshore open boat fishing and cod fishing, there was a tendency for Burra to lead the way in innovation, and a Burra crew acquired one of the first luggers in 1876.[32] Although it was normal practice for the buying of boats to be financed by merchants and herring curers, who generally retained an interest in the boats, in Burra the proportion of shore owners was generally lower than elsewhere. It was also in Burra that the only true fishing village in Shetland grew up in the 1880s and 1890s. The principal reason behind the establishment of Hamnavoe (Fig. 2.3B) was its greater accessibility to the haddock and herring fishing grounds, compared with the 'south end' of the island. This favourable location had been earlier associated with the establishment of cod fishing stations, and up to three herring stations in the 1880s, but there had been virtually no settlement. It was an indicator of the changed socio-economic conditions of the fishermen that, as the herring fishing and haddock fishing expanded, they began to move from the south end and settle in Hamnavoe.

The position of the areas possessing substantial numbers of decked boats was further strengthened economically by their participation in the spring-line fishing for cod and ling, using the herring boats and occasionally the cod smacks, although these boats operated mainly from stations in the northern half of the islands, far removed from the home base of the fishermen. The great depression in the Shetland herring fishing in the late 1880s and early 1890s, consequent upon a series of poor fishings, and reinforced by a decline in spring-line fishing because of competition from trawlers, tended to hit the peripheral areas hardest, as by this time the haaf fishing also was in steep decline. The centres depending upon the fishing all-year-round (notably Burra, Scalloway and Sandwick) tended to strengthen their position economically as centres of investment by fishermen and merchants in the new, larger 'fifie' * and 'zulu' * herring boat models in the late 1890s and early 1900s. However, the new pattern cannot be fully understood unless account is taken of the increasing importance of the winter haddock fishing in the months from November to February.

As in the case of the first phase of expansion in the herring fishing, which it paralleled, the haddock fishing was fairly widely distributed, especially in the core area near the haddock fishing grounds of the Fetlar Firth, Yell Sound, east of the South Mainland and in the Burra Haaf. In the case of the fresh fish market, the availability of steamer connections was important in order to get the fish to market. In the winter months, the principal connections were with Lerwick and Scalloway only. Thus haddocks from the remoter northern areas fetched prices a little over half those in areas accessible to the steamer terminals.[33] Those areas which were fortunate enough to be relatively near to the grounds, and to have strong fishing traditions, were again favoured. Burra and Scalloway were especially prominent, as the Burra Haaf was by the richest haddock fishing area. The haddock fishing in the northern central region, and in the peripheral districts, tended to decline in the 1890s, along with the economy of these areas generally, while in the favoured central areas of Burra, Scalloway, Lerwick (where haddock fishing was established by immigrants from the Moray Firth coastlands), and to a lesser extent Whalsay and Skerries, this fishing was a strong asset which permitted fishing all year round, although small open boats were still adhered to, and the herring boats were laid up in winter.

By the end of the period, therefore, Burra had emerged as the leading fishing district in Shetland, with Scalloway, Whalsay and Lerwick of lesser, but significant importance. In addition, Sandwick and Whiteness were important herring boat-owning localities, but tended to decline with the demise of the sailboats after 1905. The influence of proximity to fishing grounds, the ability to fish all year round, and the tendency for greater economic dependence to be placed upon the fishing, had gradually built up strong fishing community traditions in these areas. The fishermen held for the first time a larger degree of initiative in the conduct of the fishing, independently of the merchants and curers. It was thus from Burra that boats first ventured to the English herring fishing, as early as 1884,[34] and to the West Coast fishing from Stornoway (Fig. 2.1), while the first fully decked motor haddock boats began to be acquired from 1909 onwards. In Burra, the fishermen even established a small co-operative for marketing haddocks in winter.[35] This independence of outlook and innovative traditions are undoubtedly key factors in the prominence of the fishing communities from 1914 to the present day, despite great technical and economic changes in which, unlike former times, proximity to grounds and agricultural considerations have played a minor role.

In conclusion, it is apparent that the development of haaf fishing, cod fishing and herring fishing before 1850 was governed by physical environmental factors and by the level of technology. It resulted in distinctive locational patterns derived in the first instance from the configuration of land and sea, and the requirement that fishing stations should be as near as possible to the fishing grounds, especially in the open-boat fishery. Thus the haaf fishery, which used open boats, dominated the peripheral area, and a certain amount of winter fishing, and the cod fishing, dominated the central region. The system of fishing tenures and truck ensured that the fishing population remained tied to the land, although the truck system as it operated in the cod fishing, in association with nearshore winter fishing, tended to favour certain of the central areas, notably on the West Side in the Scalloway and Burra districts.

The movement towards ownership of boats by the fishermen, which encouraged the fishing communities to develop in the latter part of the nineteenth century, was made possible by the decline of the truck system, and the institution of a system of agreements between the fishermen on the one hand and the merchants and curers on the other. After 1870, the change to haddock and herring fishing strongly favoured the inshore areas which had taken part in the earlier winter fishings. The herring fishing boat ownership tended to be pioneered in areas from which the haddock fishing was being prosecuted. Although ownership of boats was widespread in the islands to begin with, it eventually became concentrated in the principal haddock fishing areas also, thus allowing complete specialisation in fishing all year round. With the exception of Scalloway, Hamnavoe and Lerwick (where the fishing community was very small), the fishermen in the rest of Burra, in Whalsay and in Skerries did not give up their land (Fig. 2.3B). Meanwhile, in the traditional haaf and cod fishing areas outside the developing fishing communities, fishing declined as the dried fish markets became less important. The decline was accelerated by their inability to exist without the truck system and subsistence agriculture.

It is a striking fact that the existing fishing communities of Shetland came into being when fishing boats were still, by and large, sail-powered, and the open boat was only beginning to be supplanted in the white fisheries by decked vessels. While it is hardly surprising that the location of communities was closely related to physical environmental characteristics, it is apparent that a combination of boat ownership and enterprise by fishermen was necessary to maintain these communities. This second characteristic is now the dominant one as proximity to grounds, because of the use of motor vessels and seine-net or purse-net fishing, is no longer an important factor.

In a British context, this lack of importance, relatively speaking, of proximity to the fishing grounds is reminiscent of the trawling industry which, using even larger vessels, is situated even further from the fishing grounds. And yet the 'traditional' community settlement patterns contrast with the social characteristics of the trawl fisheries, which are based in large towns such as Grimsby, Hull and

Aberdeen. Although having important 'traditional' antecedents, the fisheries date from the closing decades of the nineteenth century. Developing at first in association with the steam trawler, the fisheries remain basically trawl fisheries. While the trawlermen form a distinct occupational class, with which they often strongly identify as individuals, they form only part of a larger urban society. Despite the fact that they may even have favoured areas of residence within the towns, there is not the close traditional connection to the local environment present in the small fishing communities. The setting up of trawler companies to exploit distant fishing grounds was much more dependent upon business enterprise than the nearness of the resource base, required in the traditional fishing areas. The large capital investment necessary favoured company-type commercial organisation rather than the often family based ownership of boats typical of the fishing village.

Notwithstanding this basic difference between the traditional fishing areas on the one hand, and the industrially organised fishing localities on the other, there are further differences even in the development of other traditional fishing communities, when compared with the Shetland case. The growth of fisheries in the Faroe Islands, for example, highlights the importance of the overall economic development in Britain from the Industrial Revolution onwards. In Faroe, which like Shetland, and indeed most areas around the northern half of the continental shelf, had a fishery based on open boats, economic development based on a cod fishery did not start until the removal of the Danish trade monopoly in 1856. The competition of this fishery was partly responsible for the decline of the Shetland smack fishery at the same time. The Faroese gained much of the expertise required from Shetland, by sailing on Shetland-owned smacks and employing Shetland skippers.

Along the western coasts of Scotland, where landowners in particular had different business interests, there was very limited development of fishing communities, such as Barra and Scalpay, although here, as elsewhere, there was much more village settlement than in Shetland. Most fishing development was based upon fishing for herring by boats from other areas. Orkney was similar in many respects, commercial agriculture being the main preoccupation of the landowners. Along the eastern coasts of Scotland, in contrast, the situation was very similar to that prevailing in Shetland. The key factor in village development of fishing communities seems to have been the economic possibilities of pursuing white fishing as well as herring fishing. In areas which were based essentially on the herring fishing, such as many Caithness, Sutherland and Easter Ross fishing villages, and some of those along the coast of Kincardine, decline set in. The most prosperous were those along the south shore of the Moray Firth, which undertook winter fishing for cod or haddocks. As in the case of Shetland, these communities tend to persist, despite great economic and technological changes. They are classic examples of cases in which the strength of family ties and community traditions, notably that of enterprise in the fisheries development, outweigh physical factors, such as proximity to the fishing grounds.

REFERENCES

1. C. A. Goodlad, *Shetland Fishing Saga*, Shetland Times, Lerwick, 1971, p. 324.
2. Hance D. Smith, 'An Historical Geography of Trade in the Shetland Islands, 1550–1914' (Univ. of Aberdeen Ph.D. thesis, Unpubl., 1972), pp. 483–8.
3. *The Shetland Times* publishes annual summaries of the economic performance of the various sectors of the Shetland economy, including production statistics.
4. Smith, op. cit., pp. 25–95.
5. Ibid., pp. 45–7.
6. Goodlad, op. cit., pp. 107–10.
7. Abstract Books. *MSS Records of the Fishery Board for Scotland, 1821–1875.* Scottish Record Office. Arthur Edmondston, *A View of the ancient and present state of the Zetland Islands*, Edinburgh, Vol. 1, 1809 p. 244.
8. Rev. George Low, *A Tour through the Islands of Orkney and Schetland in 1774.* Edinburgh, 1879, pp. 95–118.
9. Edmondston, op. cit., p. 283.
10. Rental of the Lordship of Zetland, Crop 1772. *MSS. Records of Hay and Co. (Lerwick) Ltd.*
11. Smith, op. cit., p. 106.
12. Ibid., pp. 106–8.
13. Ibid., pp. 111–14.
14. Rental of the Lordship of Zetland, op. cit.
15. Edmondston, op. cit., Vol. 1, pp. 298–9.
16. Notes by Thomas Mouat of Garth from *The Wealth of Nations, Vol. 1*, pp. 215–16. In: Notebook, *Gardie MSS.*

17. J. Shand, 'Foreign Coin in Shetland', *Old Lore Misc. of Orkney, Shetland, Caithness and Sutherland*, Vol. 6, 1913, 37–40.
18. Edmondston, op. cit., Vol. 1, pp. 294–305.
19. *Report of Her Majesty's Commissioners of Inquiry into the condition of the crofters and cotters in the Highlands and Islands of Scotland* (1884). H.M.S.O., Edinburgh. *Vol. II, Minutes of Evidence*, pp. 1300–1. Smith, op. cit., pp. 227–9.
20. Letter Books, Collector to Board, 1971 et seq. *MSS Records of H.M. Customs & Excise*, Customs House, Lerwick, contain the fullest accounts of cod fishing stations.
21. Smith, op. cit., pp. 214–15.
22. Edmondston, op. cit., Vol. 1, pp. 312–13.
23. Smith, op. cit., pp. 201–7.
24. Articles of Agreement for the Cod Fishing, 1824 and 1890. *E. S. Reid Tait Collection*, Shetland County Library.
25. Numerous records of eviction notices, styled: Summonses for Removal, are among material presently being catalogued in the Records of Lerwick Sheriff Court, by Mr. Brian Smith.
26. Goodlad, op. cit., pp. 182–4.
27. Smith, op. cit., pp. 276–89.
28. The first cargo of foreign grain was imported into Shetland on 14 June 1861, from Copenhagen, according to a note in a large bound volume containing records of arrivals and sailings of vessels, 1834–1837, and 1859–1861 in *MSS Records of Hay & Co. (Lerwick) Ltd.*
29. *Annual Report of the Fishery Board for Scotland*, 1905, p. 242.
30. Goodlad, op. cit., pp. 20–31.
31. Register of Fishing Vessels, 1869 et seq. *MSS Records. H.M. Customs & Excise*, Custom House, Lerwick.
32. A. Halcrow, *The Sail Fishermen of Shetland*, Lerwick, 1950, p. 135.
33. *The Shetland Times*, 10 March 1888, 31 December 1904. *Annual Report of the Fishery Board for Scotland, 1905*, p. 213.
34. *The Shetland Times*, 4 October 1884.
35. *Report of the Scottish Departmental Committee on the North Sea Fishing Industry*, H.M.S.O., London, 1914, pp. 212–13.

GLOSSARY

Words marked with an asterisk in the text have been included here.

baukt This was a length of line convenient in long-line fishing. In the haaf fishing, it was often 50 fathoms long, with hooks spaced at intervals of 5 fathoms. The haddock fishing also used a system of baukts, such as three lines each with six baukts used by each man in the Burra district. The baukts were tied together as the lines were laid.

booth Merchant's depot or trade point.

fifie A straight stemmed sailing lugger of a design used in Fife.

fourern A four-oared double-ended, clinker-built open boat, similar, but not identical, to the Norwegian *faering*, hence the name. Keel length was in the order of 14 feet.

haaf open sea; cognate of Norwegian *hav*, sea or ocean.

piltock coalfish (i.e. young saithe).

sixern A six-oared double-ended, clinker built open boat, similar but not identical to the Norwegian *seksaering*. Keel length was from 18 feet to 22 feet. The nineteenth-century sixerns tended to be larger than their eighteenth-century counterparts.

smack A sailing vessel rigged fore and aft with one or two masts, a gaff mainsail and bowsprit.

tack A lease, in this case of land, or fishing stations.

tacksman A lease, or middleman, who leased land or fishings from a landowner, collected the rent and/or carried on the fish trade, paying the landowner a certain sum for the privilege, known as tack duty.

toms Snoods, or short lengths of line attached to the long-line. The hooks were tied to the toms.

voe A Shetland dialect word applied to an inlet of the sea.

zulu A sailing lugger from the east coast of Scotland which was larger than the 'fifie'.

Three · A Sociological Study of an Italian Community of Fishermen

BERNARDO CATTARINUSSI*

INTRODUCTION

The following analysis of the development of a community of fisher-men is intended to verify the hypothesis that technological changes not only influence labour organisation but also family structure, political and religious attitudes and, in general, the prevailing value system.

The community studied is a little village, Marano Lagunare, located on the Upper Adriatic Sea, between Venice and Trieste. The environment of the fishermen is a lagoon divided from the sea by a succession of littoral sand bars and islets. Several channels permit access to the lagoon.

Various research methods were employed in the study. After an examination of the literature on the traditional organisation of fishing in the lagoon, the method of observer participation was used. The author joined in the daily life of the community, shared the hard work of the fishermen and attended meetings and discussions on fishing and fishermen. A questionnaire was also submitted to a sample of fifty fishermen to verify the hypothesis drawn from the literature analysis and from observer participation.

TRADITIONAL ORGANISATION OF THE COMMUNITY

The community of Marano Lagunare was governed by regulations which went back to the fifteenth century. The community was divided into 'great companies', formed by more than ten fishermen, and 'little companies', formed by a smaller numbers. In addition, there were independent fishermen. Only those who were born and

* I wish to express my special thanks to Bruno Tellia, Franco Demarchi, Anna Maria Boileau and Roberto Facini of the Institute of International Sociology of Gorizia for their valuable comments and suggestions.

resident in the village had the right to fish in the lagoon. The community was directed by a leader, called 'deputy of the fishermen', who had the authority to judge the conflicts arising in fishing.

According to the different methods of fishing, the year was divided into six seasons. At the beginning of every season the great companies drew lots for a fishing area in the lagoon. They had the right of fishing by placing, before sunrise, a *cogol* (cylindrical net divided into six sectors by wooden hoops) on the fishing area. The little companies had the right of fishing by setting, after sunrise, a *grisiol* (a trap of woven marshy reeds) on the places still free. Finally, the independent fisherman fixed nets without formalities.

Every fisherman had an equality of gear since the number, form and size were prescribed, and if nets were used, these were required to be of the prescribed mesh. In winter only fishing with naked arms and with harpoon was allowed. These rules and other more detailed ones tried chiefly to preserve the different species of fish.

A company was formed when some fishermen gave each other their word to fish together for one season. The company was given the name of the leader. A fisherman who broke his word was rejected during that season by all the other companies.

Every member of the company possessing gear received one 'part' of the earnings, the others a 'half part'; the children from five to ten received 'according to their merit' from 5 to 25 per cent of the earnings. If a member of the company was taken ill during the season, he received his part of the earnings as if he had worked; if he fell ill before the fishing season, the company co-operated with the family in the preparation of the gear. If the whole company was hard pressed for money, the chief borrowed the necessary amount. Each week the fishermen gave a certain part of their earnings to the poorest. During the year some special catches were made for the same reason.[1]

Living conditions were extremely hard. The fishermen sailed on Monday mornings in their rowing-boats and came back on the following Saturday or Sunday. Earnings were meagre; they placed the fisherman in a condition of static poverty. Two surveys carried out by the International Labour Organisation in the post-war period illustrate that these conditions were almost the same in several countries.[2] A survey carried out in the ports of the upper Adriatic Sea in 1958 showed that the average family of six persons, two of whom were able to work and four were dependent, was barely capable of satisfying the primary necessities of life and survived with a half-kilo of fish per day.

FISHING CO-OPERATION

The fishermen were caught between the risks of the sea and those of market forces. In some seaports the fishermen were at the mercy of middle men who used to sell on credit all the tools necessary for fishing and bought the fish at an usurious price. In order to protect the fishermen from exploitation and to let the fishermen adjust themselves to modern fishing conditions at a time when motorisation of the boats began, it was thought useful to create co-operative societies. A certain degree of solidarity was part of the tradition of the communities of fishermen, and had proved necessary in surmounting the difficulties posed by an unstable market and food shortages. New co-operative societies arose with very different purposes and organisations. On one hand, some societies supplied the fishermen with the tools necessary for equipping the boats and with fuel; on the other, some contributed to the organisation of the market.[3]

The importance of the co-operative societies varies to a high degree. In Italy and Spain in the 1960s the co-operative societies managed 75 per cent of all the catches. Outside Europe, the most important co-operative movement is the Japanese, which handles about 65 per cent of the catch. The main field of co-operative development has been confined to enterprises of medium and small scale in Europe, North America, Japan and Australia, whereas co-operation has not grown to any extent among the fishermen of the developing countries. Another group of fishermen who seldom join co-operative societies are those who work in continental waters.[4]

Along Italian shores the first expressions of solidarity had mainly a religious content and were later devoted to the assistance of the poor. The first confraternities among fishermen, besides attending to religious festivals, carried out some forms of co-operative ventures at Trapani, Naples and Venice. The development of early systems of co-operative organisations in the eighteenth and nineteenth centuries was due to the pressure of the industrial economy.

The early efforts were addressed to the better organisation of the product sale. Later on the efforts were addressed to the joint purchase of boat-building materials, and the necessity of assistance and social security was felt. The co-operation among fishermen advanced in the first half of this century particularly along Sicilian, Calabrian and

Venetian shores. During the twenty years of Fascism in Italy the co-operative societies were subjected to a strong control by the State. After the Second World War the control function was led back within the boundaries useful for voluntary co-operative associations.[5]

The Co-operative Society of Fishermen at Marano Lagumare

The fishermen of Marano Lagunare formed a limited-liability co-operative society in 1951. This society attends to the purchase of the fishing materials (nets, rigging, cases, paint, diesel oil and so on), to the sale of the product by means of contracts with industrial and commercial enterprises and to the management of the services needed for freezing fish.

Fishermen aged from eighteen to sixty are members of the co-operative society. When a member is over sixty he may continue working on the lagoon, but he pays a lower precentage on the fish caught (5 per cent instead of the 10 per cent of the members) to cover market expenses and insurance premiums. Thus, the problems of retirement are not found in the Marano Lagunare community. Physical strength has in the fishing field an importance equal to the acquisition of experience. With the unrelenting advance of the years the fisherman becomes an important example to the younger men and devotes himself to a less tiring fishery. His work is no less valuable, since he is skilled—for example, in the repairing of nets. Retirement does not lead to the loss of social contacts in the work and residential milieux, which are often regarded by sociologists as a source of anomie.

From a legal point of view the members of the co-operative society are divided into two groups; the first includes those who practise the so-called 'little fishery', the second those practising the 'great fishery'. The little fishery is carried out with a boat suited to coastal fishing (5–7 metres in length); the great fishery is carried out with bigger boats (7–9 metres in length).

One kind of deep-sea fishing is carried on with *lamparas* * at night; another is trawling. Every boat tows two cutters with the lamparas and boat and cutters place themselves in a triangle. If the prospects are good—that is, if the fish surface and start to turn in whirls under the lights—the fishing continues. After two hours the cutters pick up the moorings and approach the boat, dragging the fish to a single point. The boat thus surrounds the fish with the net and the fish

---

* A form of purse seine used with very bright lights.

can be sorted during the return to port. The boats arrive in port about 6 a.m., when the wives are getting up to take the children to school or to go to work.[6]

Trawling is carried on by day. The departure is at 4 a.m.; the trawl is hauled three or four times until the afternoon. On the lagoon different hours correspond to every kind of fishery. Common hours, 5 a.m. and 4 p.m., correspond to the sale of the fish, which is carried out by auction.

The number of fishermen belonging to the great fishery since the Second World War has always been far below the number of lagoon fishermen, in spite of the arrival of immigrant deep-sea fishermen from Yugoslavia. The total number of fishermen in the community in the last decades has diminished, as Table 3.1 shows. It is a trend comparable to the flight of the peasant from agriculture. Deep-sea fishing was particularly hit. The decrease in fishing on the lagoon is partially explicable by the enormous damage caused by industrial pollution.

The analysis of the volume of fish sales in the last ten years shows that the total income of the fishermen has nearly doubled (Table 3.2). We can reasonably suppose that the reasons for the decrease in fishermen are not only economic; they include social factors such as the need for social prestige, for leisure, for cultural development, for living a life more relevant to modern social experience, or for sickness and disablement insurance. It is not a question of social mobility peculiar to those who change position in the occupation, but of occupational mobility from changes in the socio-economic environment. Some of the fishermen found employment in local industry while others emigrated. Difficulties for former fishermen in finding work derive from an occupational and environmental leap, coupled with the problems of the integration of unskilled labour into modern industry ashore.

If we divide the fishermen into age-groups, we observe that in the last twenty years there has been a strong senescence in the occupation (Tables 3.3–4). We can see a progressive flight of the young people and a decrease of those over sixty. Retirement of old people is probably caused by the improvement of social assistance. In the questionnaire submitted to the sample of fishermen was included this question: 'Why do you think young people leave the fishery?'. Half of the fishermen answered, 'Because it is a trade which imposes too many sacrifices.' Others pointed out as a reason for the move from fishing the fatiguing work (12), the lack of leisure time (8), the meagre

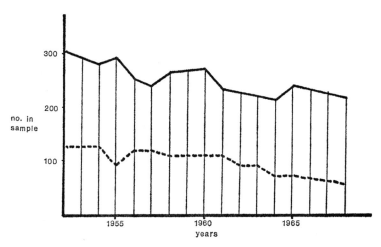

TABLE 3.1 *Number of fishermen engaged in fishing in the Great Companies (– – –) and Little Companies between 1952 and 1968 in Marano Lagunare.*

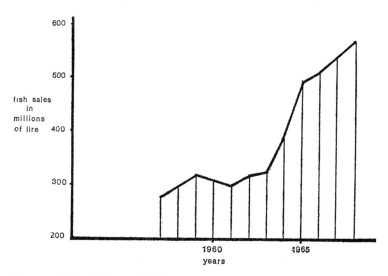

TABLE 3.2 *Value of fish catches (in millions of lire) between 1957 and 1968 in Marano Lagunare.*

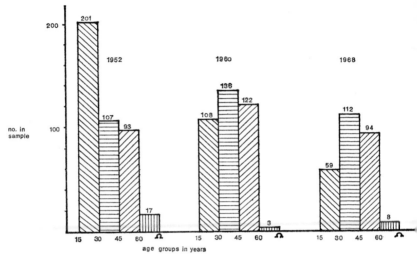

TABLE 3.3 *Number of fishermen in selected age groups fishing from Marano Lagunare in 1952, 1960 and 1968.*

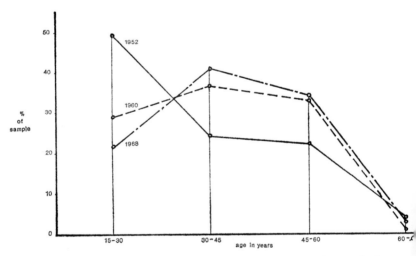

TABLE 3.4 *Age of fishermen: trends of age in the work-force in 1952, 1960 and 1968 in Marano Lagunare.*

earnings, the very bad conditions of work, lack of future prospects and the low prestige status. The autostereotype regarding this last point is confirmed by several surveys on occupational prestige, while the reference to the meagre earnings reveals the internalisation of the heterostereotype.

IMPACT OF THE NEW TECHNOLOGY

Technological development, which replaced the toil of rowing with the noisy but effective engine, and which created nylon nets more resistant to salt water than hemp and marsh reed nets, played a determined role in the decline of the rules concerning fishing on the lagoon and in the transformation of the collective structure.

The fishermen no longer leave in their various groups or companies on Monday mornings to return on Saturday or Sunday. Their huts, which once acted as temporary domiciles when weather conditions did not let them sleep in their boats, act now as storage for tools or as tourist attractions.

The companies disappeared and with them the role of the fishermen who plied between the port, the fishing grounds and the market place, and brought victuals and news to those who remained on the lagoon. The group widened when the birth clause was removed. Fishermen mastered new fishing methods through contacts with other communities and with other fishermen.

For a certain period the phenomenon of social displacement of the techniques prevailed, the displacement between the time when findings are available to the time of their appliance, which may be deferred for reasons of social order. In this case, displacement could be attributed to the lack of financial means. The constitution of the co-operative society served to nullify this displacement. Consequently, a short-sighted and more intense exploitation of the sea resources took place through the use of gear once rigorously forbidden or allowed only in particular periods, with a gradual impoverishment of the marine fauna.

Technological development contributed to the reduction of the physical aspects of the fisherman's work. The arrival of motor vessels reduced travelling time. Innovations in plastics and rubber materials supplied the fishermen with diving-suits and other coverings in resistant materials. The most stressful aspect, which still remains, was that work time did not mesh with that of the daily rhythm of life ashore.

This situation leads girls to consider the fisherman to be of mediocre value in the matrimonial market. The reluctance of girls to marry fishermen is confirmed by a lot of marriages between native girls and foreign young men. 'The girls,' said a fisherman, 'are free in the evening, whereas I spend the evenings and the nights near the lamparas with the nets and the fishes.'

Fishing is no longer carried on in collaboration by groups of 40–50 members. Crews are now composed of two or three men for fishing in the lagoon and of four or six men for deep-sea fishing. In these groups social control is exercised by those who know the skills of the job. This form of control is cemented by friendship, by identification with the norms and by a high degree of communication. The members of a group of small size, by assuming the responsibility for the activity, do not feel themselves to be like wheels in a mechanism they cannot control; technical and organising problems which develop for the group in action are everybody's responsibility.

In the fishing community studied, the industrial sociologist's concern with the problems of the alienated worker does not have a counterpart. The fisherman does not suffer from frustration caused by a constraint towards himself; the fishermen are free to organise their work with a great deal of autonomy, and income is divided among the members of the crew without great discordances. In the great fishery 40 per cent of the catch belongs to the boat; that is, to those who own the boat and provide for the cost of fuel and maintenance, while in the little fishery there is one part of the catch for each member of the crew and one for the boat.

Technological development has increased the leisure time of the fisherman. Traditionally, when the fishing started on Monday and finished on Saturday, the fisherman spent the time ashore getting drunk and 'begetting a son'. Nowadays the time free from work activities (hauls, fishing, sale of the product, cleaning and mending nets) has increased with the use of powerful engines and through the introduction of stronger nets. In spite of the technological improvement, though, the inn has remained the most popular place for the fisherman. Nevertheless, the leisure time of the fisherman is undoubtly smaller than that of the majority of urban workers which is calculated to be 20–30 hours a week and to which we must add three weeks of annual holidays. We should note, however, the periods of compelled inactivity caused by weather changes (wind, rain, frost), by moon phases (fishing with lamparas, for instance, cannot be carried on during moonlight) and by the biological cycles of the fish.

If we go back to the current tripartition of leisure's functions (recuperation, amusement and development of the personality), we could say that for the fisherman the first is essential. The function of amusement expresses itself normally in activities tied to the great influence exercised by mass media. With the third function of leisure, the development of the personality through gathering and voluntary participation in the life of various social groups, we observed that 'cultural renunciation' was applicable to many fishermen. To the question, 'How and with whom do you spend Sunday afternoons?', three-quarters of the fishermen said that friends were leisure partners, while only a quarter spent Sunday afternoons with their families. Some recuperate by resting, others play cards or watch a football match, while others stroll through the village.

To the question, 'Do you participate in any voluntary associa-tion?', only 18 subjects answered affirmatively. This tendency not to become members of voluntary associations in the village com-munities is confirmed by some recent enquiries.[8] One of these, carried out by the Institute of International Sociology of Gorizia, Italy, showed that the presence of voluntary associations appears almost as a function of the demographical dimensions of the community.[9] A degree of political indifference was also found among the young fishermen, who, rather than on the theories of the three M's of student protest (Marx, Mao, Marcuse), build their lives on other values (work, wife, car).[10]

Even the questions about mass media were concerned with leisure. To the question, 'Do you read newspapers and magazines?', only twelve fishermen who were interviewed said they read newspapers every day, while only ten regularly read magazines. All the fishermen interviewed have television at home, but only twelve see the pro-grammes every evening, whereas most of them switch on the television sometimes or rarely. Therefore the television does not have the same influence among the fishermen that it exerts in other contexts.

Because of the longer time spent ashore and the growth of income, we observed a marked improvement in the fishermen's housing. The houses of the community lost the distinctive marks of poverty and unsanitary conditions, while malaria and other epidemics are no longer a problem and survive only in the votive prayers of the community. If there is still danger in the life of the fishermen, it is due to storms or the lack of mastery of new technologies.

THE FAMILY OF THE FISHERMAN

A study of the family in the community was conducted to ascertain whether there was a clear decline of the family as an economic unity and if there was a spread of the attitude similar to that which the American sociologist E. C. Banfield, in his research on a little rural village of southern Italy, labelled 'amorale familism'. The general rule of the inhabitants of this village was: 'maximise the material and immediate profits of the kinship group by supposing that the others act in the same way'.[11]

This study of the community of Marano Lagunare has supplied us with strong evidence that the family of the fisherman is no longer an economic unit. This is confirmed by the non-inheritance of the fishing occupation and by the reduced size of the families, a phenomenon which also has been shown for the rural family.[12]

The birth of sons does not correspond to the need for manpower on the fishing boat and the generative act is extraneous to all calculations of investment on the part of the family. Most of the married women work, and young children are looked after at the kindergarten. Recently it has been possible for young men to continue their studies up to university level. The girls, too, are leaving the family, seeking the autonomy of earnings as industrial workers rather than the domestic life of the family home.

The composition of the families of the fishermen interviewed was as follows:

TABLE 3.5 *Size of fishermen's families in Marano Lagunare*

Number in family	Number of families	%
2	5	10
3	10	20
4	9	18
5	9	18
6	8	16
7	5	10
8	1	2
9	2	4
10	1	2
TOTALS	50	100%

To the question, 'Do you think that your work lets you devote yourself to your family and to your children's upbringing?', 68 per cent of the fishermen answered affirmatively, whereas 32 per cent admitted that their work allowed them only a short time to spend with their families.

To observe whether it was possible to emphasise the attitude of 'amorale familism', this question was asked: 'Trawling and fishing with harpoons spoils the bottom of the lagoon. Do you think that your colleagues carry on these kinds of fishing to better their families' living conditions?' This question was later defined in these terms: 'Do you think that a fisherman should carry on a kind of fishing which damages other fishermen to increase family income?' Of the subjects interviewed 84 per cent answered affirmatively. This could be considered an index of a tendency to maximise the profits of the family group, regardless of the damage to the rest of the community. This attitude is attributable to the communal memory of former poverty and to enormous damage caused by industrial pollution.

POLITICAL AND RELIGIOUS ATTITUDES

All the surveys on political attitudes of fishermen point out that they normally vote for leftist parties. American sociologists consider this a result of the economic insecurity of groups of workers.[13] This general political attitude seems to be in contrast with the attitude of the fishermen considered as a community. In reality the results of the last political elections show a clear prevalence for a party of the centre, the Christian Democratic Party. The hypothesis, which affirms that a high degree of attachment to traditional values diverts impoverished workers from leftist political action, seems therefore confirmed.

Mass media do not play an important role in the political choice. In effect, the kind of work with hours that are far different from those of the normal daily rhythm prevents the fisherman from exposing himself to news telecasts, shown mainly in late evening; beside, as we have seen, magazines and newspapers are rarely read. Consequently, the fisherman does not appear to have much political information related to his particular problems and is rigid in his choice of a party of which he has no exact knowledge. Thus we can expect any open contrast between the positions of the party supported and those of the fisherman.

In regard to religious attitude and behaviour, we can also observe that the religious practice of the fishermen is very strong, bound to the traditional forms of faith and which persist when the fishermen emigrate.

CONCLUSIONS

The hypothesis posed at the beginning of this research into an Italian community of fishermen was that the introduction of a new technology wrought changes not only on the outward aspect of the community but also on the value system.

With reference to the first aspect, we have already seen that technological development gave rise to a different organisation of the fisherman's work. The arrival of engines and synthetic materials, by shortening the times of voyages and by making the fishing tools more durable, caused the decline of the companies, those co-operative groups of 30–40 members who carried on the fishing in the lagoon in common and who joined together at the beginning of every fishing season. With the companies also disappeared the figure of the fishermen who plied between the village and the place on the lagoon where his colleagues were fishing. In particular, the length of time at sea has changed as the companies left on Mondays and came back on Saturdays to fish at distances that the present boats cover in about two hours. Work collectivities are now reduced to groups in one or two boats.

Technological improvements have also increased the leisure time of the fisherman, but he does not make use of it as predicted by the sociologists of leisure. Innovations have also caused the decline of detailed rules regarding fishing in the different seasons which aimed to protect fish species, and have led to an intense and, in many ways, irrational exploitation of the sea resouces.

The creation of the co-operative society has speeded this trans-formation. It played an important role in the organisation of the fishermen and in the advantages offered to them.[14] Nevertheless, it was not able to slow the migration of young men, who are leaving the fishery because of reasons we cannot attribute merely to an economic matrix.

We found among the fishermen an attitude we could define as a certain degree of 'amorale familism' that partially replaced the spirit of mutual co-operation and assistance, even if there are signs of change towards a less particularistic orientation. The picture of the fisherman which loomed out of the enquiry is of a workman rough, patient, tied to traditions and equipped with an intimate religiousness that allows him to turn his eyes to heaven not only to observe weather changes.

REFERENCES

1. R. Olivotto, *Marano Lagunare: Volo attraverso i Secoli*, Cividale, 1892.
2. Bureau International du Travail, *Les Conditions de Travail dans l'Industrie de la Peche. Geneve*, 1952.
   Bureau International du Travail, *Les Conditions de Travail des Pecheurs*, Geneve, 1958.
3. P. Lacour, 'Les Associations Yolontaires dans la Peche Maritime Francaise', *Archives Internationales de Sociologie de la Co-operation*, No. 3, 1963.
4. M. Digby, *La Cooperacion entre Pescadores*. Holanda, 1961.
5. E. Ciuffa, *La Cooperazione Peschereccia in Italia*, 1953.
6. P. Fortuna, 'Una Notte in Mare con i Pescatori di Marano', *Julia Gens*, 1961.
7. G. Friedmann, P. Naville, *Traite de Sociologie du Travail*, Paris, 1961.
8. B. Tellia, 'L'Associazionismo Giovanile', in F. Demarchi *et al.* (eds.): *Gioventu 1970 nel Friuli-Venezia Giulia*, Trieste, 1971.
9. F. Demarchi, *L'Associazionismo in provincia di Gorizia*, Forni, Bologna, 1970.
10. B. Tellia, 'Alcuni Modelli Occidentali della Ribellione Giovanile', *Prospettive di Efficienza*, No. 3, 1969.
11. E. C. Banfield, *The Moral Basis of a Backward Society*, The Free Press, Glencoe, Ill., 1958.
    F. Demarchi, *Societa e Spazio*, Istituto Superiore di Scienze Sociali, Trento, 1969.
12. C. Barberis, Sociologia Murale, Bologna, 1965.
13. S. M. Lipset, P. F. Lazarsfeld, A. M. Barton & J. Linz, 'The Psychology of Voting: an Analysis of Political Behaviour', in G. Lindsey (ed.), *Handbook of Social Psychology*, Cambridge University Press, Cambridge, 1954.
14. M. Garano, 'I Pescatori di Marano', *La Cooperazione del Friuli-Venezia Giulia*, No. 2, 1968.

Four · Resource Management and Spatial Competition in Newfoundland Fishing: An Exploratory Essay

RAOUL ANDERSEN AND GEOFFREY STILES

INTRODUCTION

This paper was developed in response to growing public and private concern in Eastern Canada, and Newfoundland in particular, over the exploitation of marine resources. Since the early 1960s, East Coast inshore and offshore fishing grounds have become the target of intensified exploitation by foreign and domestic fishing operations, ranging from migratory herring-seiners to large, highly organised dragger fleets numbering upwards of seventy vessels. For the Newfoundlander, in particular, intensification has meant a number of things, situated as he is beside one of the world's great fishing grounds: if he is an offshore man, it has meant more risk in his own operation due to increased crowding in major fishing areas, and gradually decreasing returns per unit effort; if he is an inshore man, these difficulties are compounded by the tangible and continuous threat of gear loss through dragger or seiner operations near the traditional inshore 'grounds'. The magnitude of change can be seen in the fact that the number of ground-fishing trawlers (50 tons and over) operating north of Cape Hatteras increased from 798 in 1959 to 1,410 in 1969.

The pressure on the resource base itself and on the 'space' which fishermen use to exploit the resource has prompted a variety of reactions in Canada. Special boards have been established to indemnify inshore fishermen for gear and catch loss in the event of dragger encroachment; enforcement procedures have been redefined and accelerated, while Canada herself attempts to persuade nations who have traditionally partaken of the local fisheries harvest to gradually phase out their rights and recognise Canadian sovereignty over sizeable portions of the continental shelf area; and most recently, an intra-industry lobby, Save Our Fisheries Association (SOFA), has been organised to increase public and government awareness of these problems.

Such reactions are not unexpected in a nation threatened, as

Canada is, by depletion of a major natural resource. But the nature and degree of these reactions suggests, to those of us who have done research in Newfoundland, a peculiarly contradictory fact: viz. that this increased awareness on the part of a 'coastal state' of its obligation to *protect* its resources, is complemented (and perhaps caused) by the desire of its own people to *arrogate* these resources to themselves. Any attempt to understand Newfoundland's fisheries, inshore *and* offshore, in terms of their approach to *resource management*, must, we feel, confront the very elementary fact that Newfoundland fishermen do *not*, as a rule, manage their *resources*, but rather manage *space*—that is, the points of privileged *access* to the resource. Lacking the biologist's information on biomass characteristics and the effects of exploitation, the fisherman's orientation is to view total resources as more or less infinite, though of course recognising that returns vary from time to time and place to place as a function of both human and non-human factors—wind, bait, tide, as well as the activities of fellow fishermen which, for the most part, are beyond their control.

By contrast, in the techno–scientific approach, fishing is seen as a 'zero-sum' game; intensified effort in one fishery implies a threat to the success of others, and the interaction between fisheries of the same or different technological types (whether or not dependent upon the same species or species-mix) is of critical concern as regards their impact on resource bases. Today, despite the increasing concern of fisheries experts, this 'ecological game' continues to be played with few rules and relatively powerless referees; there is little effective effort to 'manage' resources in the sense of husbanding them to achieve optimal sustainable yields. The sorry plight of the international whale 'fishery', and salmon and haddock fisheries in the Northwest Atlantic, are cases in point.

It is one of the fundamental assumptions of this paper that this techno–scientific model of fishing and marine resources—an objectively accurate model, despite its failure to provoke restraint—ought not be confused with that taken by fishermen themselves. Our research suggests that most Newfoundland fishermen have engaged in competition for resources only in a relative sense; specifically, they have been concerned with the production levels attained by other units in their immediate socio-spatial environment—and their reaction to these problems has always been articulated in terms of spatial factors, i.e. they have husbanded exploitative opportunities rather than resources *per se*.

It is our purpose in this paper to explore the nature and limits of the application of such 'resource management' (*vis-á-vis* spatial management) in traditional Newfoundland fishing, and beyond that to analyse the kinds of contemporary events which may influence this phenomenon, so that we may more adequately understand the recent reactions by fishermen and industry to the exploitative threats of 'outsiders'.

HISTORICAL BACKGROUND

In Newfoundland, and presumably in the Northwest Atlantic in general, fishing units in the same techno–economic sector have been competitive primarily where *spatial positioning* or access to the resource is concerned (e.g. see Kipling's description of dory fishing on the Grand Banks in the late 1800s and cf. Andersen's description of competition in modern Grand Banks trawler fishing, 1972). In Newfoundland, *inshore* fishing was carried on in waters immediately adjacent to small communities. Local fishermen in each community vied with each other for places in 'their' local waters. In *offshore* fishing, on the other hand, individual schooners equipped with dories competed with each other for the best locations on the Grand Banks and other important offshore areas.

In practice, the inshore and offshore fisheries were viewed by fishermen as relatively discrete sectors of the Newfoundland saltfish trade. Each sector had independent spheres of manpower, capital, ownership and management, and separate temporal–spatial routines. The points of interaction between these sectors were *complementary* rather than competitive. Both supplied saltfish to distant foreign markets, revenues from which sustained the flow of subsistence goods and other essential services to the smallest outports. The production and support operations of the offshore fishery also represented a source of (1) seasonal employment and/or supplementary income for those participating in the inshore fishery, or (2) permanent employment for many who decided to seek a living outside the inshore fishery. An additional point of articulation, particularly in the nineteenth century, was the so-called 'Bait Trade', in which inshore operators procured herring, capelin and squid by their own means and sold them directly to foreign 'bankers' (Cheeseman *et al.* 1957; Innis 1954).

In the earliest years of Newfoundland's settlement this complementarity was minimised by British restrictions on the development of inshore, settlement-based fishing. At this time, inshore fisheries were seen as competitive for *manpower* with the offshore, since the latter were primarily viewed as a vehicle for the training of future seamen, whose value to the Crown was lost if they settled on the island for purposes of local fishing (Graham 1967). This resulted in deliberate, though rarely successful, attempts to restrict settlement and thereby choke off the developing inshore industry, which was based on small-boat operations and run by diversified local entrepreneurs who were not tied to specific mercantile interests (1971). It was not until after the Napoleonic Wars, when some of the larger, mercantile firms withdrew their interests in the offshore fishery, that the inshore sector began to develop on an enlarged scale, eventually resulting in somewhat closer integration with the offshore sector (Innis 1954).

Some more subtle elements of competition did exist between the two sectors. Thus, for example, when some schooner operators specialising in the offshore fishery developed large-scale saltfish curing operations, such as those on specially prepared beaches at Grand Bank, and imposed more rigorous quality and grading standards, competition ensued between the large and the small outport producers—but this competition was chiefly over price in the Newfoundland market; it had nothing to do with a sense of competition between inshore and offshore operators over the resource itself. On the whole, then, offshore and inshore sectors engaged in open competition for fishing *space*, though occasionally they did contend for other factors of production. The following section elaborates some of these points with respect to (*a*) the inshore fishery and (*b*) the offshore fishery.

TRADITIONAL SYSTEMS OF COGNITION AND SPATIAL CONTROL

The Inshore Fishery

In the traditional inshore sector, where kin-based (see e.g. Firestone 1967; Faris 1966; Nemec 1972) fishing units employ handlines, trawls (long-lines), gillnets and stationary 'traps', inter-unit competition centres on spatial access. 'Fish' is synonymous with cod, the key resource (Faris 1966, p. 32). It is seen as essentially unlimited in that the *total* biomass is not seen as directly affected by local fishing effort. If cod fails to appear in economically significant numbers in a given year, this is explained by the view that 'they must have gone someplace else'. The seasonal and annual coming and going of cod, evidenced by periodic fluctuations in catch, are seen as responses to climatic and oceanographic factors over which man has no control and little knowledge. When the cod do appear, however, fishermen seem to be acutely aware of the effects of other fishermen's activities on their own returns. They engage in a zero-sum game with respect to *local* resources and *local* competitors, and they devise long- and short-term competitive strategies based on rights to specific 'berths' or portions of the fishing grounds.

The characteristic dory and/or trap boat technology, even after boats were motorised and sail and human power was largely displaced, confined the fisherman of each outport to his 'own' nearby waters. The first gasoline engines were introduced in 1904, and most fishermen had engines by about 1915, but these were too low powered to permit an increase in boat size. Inshore trap-boats remained limited to a length of about 25 feet until about 1958, when diesel engines were introduced. Because of the ever present danger of sudden weather changes, fishermen had to operate within one or two hours of shore and safety; they had little opportunity to encroach upon the fishing grounds of another community. And where such encroachment did become possible in later years, the trespass was responded to by united opposition from the offended fishermen. The offender could be sanctioned directly and effectively. A few boat loads of rocks, dumped into a trap which has been set in an unused berth in another community's waters, is a most effective form of communication!

Fishermen in each community placed high value upon maintenance of equal opportunity to points of resource-access, but individual fishermen strove to build their technical expertise and knowledge of fish behaviour, oceanographic characteristics and positional co-ordinates, and treated this often hard-gained information as scarce capital (see e.g. Faris 1966, pp. 34–36; Lofgren 1972; Nemec 1972; Stiles 1972a; and cf. Andersen 1972; Paine 1957). The greatest amount of eco-spatial competition in fishing centred on being first in effectively positioning the more mobile techniques employed, e.g. handlines, trawls and gillnets.

Working from day to day through each season, the first man to set his gear in a 'trawl' (long-line) fishery controlled a location with a radius determined by experience and custom. There is the implication that success would be fairly evenly distributed among fishermen so engaged over a given season. Thus Faris suggests that the 'men shift about and "all hands" usually manage to get one or more decent "spots" during the course of the cod wanderings' (1966, p. 32). On the other hand, the winter inshore codfishery on the island's southwest coast, studied by Stiles (1972b), appears to have been characterised by striking differences in catch per unit. The densest stocks could be found around the 90-fathom line, corresponding to the 'edge of the shelf' in that area. Boats with larger engines or better sailing characteristics (in the days when sail was still a frequent alternative) consistently reached their preferred grounds first—and, therefore, tended to have higher average catches. In an effort to counter these purely mechanical advantages, fishermen engaged in a perpetual guessing-game over the time of departure to the grounds. This often reached comical extremes: men were known to mask their oil lamps on arising, tiptoe down to the wharf in their 'worsteds' (wool socks) and 'slip the lines before anyone knew they were gone'!

Stationary gear such as the cod trap is placed for an entire season (the Labrador 'floater' codfishery excepted; see Black 1960) at great risk and investment. Thus effective use requires a rough scale of the relative advantage of different locations ('berths') in nearby waters. Many communities developed such a scale of spatial advantages after years of experience. In the early years of cod trap use (1880s), however, positioning followed the pattern set by the more traditional and mobile techniques: the first man to set his trap in a given location held the location for the season or until the trap was moved (whether intentionally or by sea action). Where there were few desirable berths and many seeking them, competition led to conflict and undesirable risks against seasonal uncertainties. One could never be certain that the last of winter storms had passed, yet one could not wait too long before berthing his trap lest someone else take the desired berth. In Old Perlican, for example, some risked placing their gear before the ice had cleared in Trinity Bay (cf. Faris 1966, p. 226). Ill-fortune often struck, and tempers flared between individuals in the competition for good berths.

Where competitive pressures and risks were high, many fishermen devised a draw for named berths in advance of each season (see e.g. Faris 1966, p. 36). In some cases, on the other hand, there was relatively little competition and berths were treated as inheritable property. Firestone (1967, pp. 93–3) speaking of berths in Savage

Cove and adjacent settlements along the Strait of Belle Isle, observed the following:

> These berths like land are obtained through patrilineal in-
> heritance and through establishing them in previously unused
> spots. In more populous areas of Newfoundland the rights
> to berths are obtained each year by lot with the most productive
> going to those who are lucky. Sandy Cove has a system in which
> berths are used in rotation by the crews in the community. In
> Savage Cove the hereditary rights to berths are respected, every-
> one being aware just where everyone's rightful berth is, some-
> times by the aid of land markers which are sighted from the
> sea. If someone is not using a berth, another can use it, but
> when the owner wants to use it no one else will. The system
> runs entirely by informal sanction.

This practice allowed a reasonable time in the early part of the season
for men to set their gear without competitive pressure from other
potential users. The initial right to compete for berth space was in
any event restricted to the local community, and vacated or temporarily unfilled berths could not be usurped by outsiders without first
obtaining local permission.

It may be noted, then, that both the annual draw and hereditary
berth rights reinforced community social and eco-spatial boundaries.
These rights are, in each case, predicated upon local residence.[2]
Both patterns were also integrative in their tendency to counter
inter-crew rivalry: given the same technology and similar expertise
and relatively equal production possibilities over time, there is less
incentive to maintain inter-crew mobility. In Old Perlican, Trinity
Bay, however, prior to adoption of a trap berth draw, men com-
mitted to one crew sometimes sought to leave for another which had
drawn a highly productive berth—sometimes by slipping out to set
their gear with that crew in the dead of night, when others would be
least likely to learn of it. In some communities on the south-west
coast, mentioned before, there was considerable inter-crew mobility
from year to year and even season to season as individual fortunes
fluctuated—though here, the absence of fixed berths made such fluctuations more common, and the advantages of a change more readily
apparent (Chiaramonte, pers. communication; and Chiaramonte
1970).

The inshore spatial-access strategies noted above apply to a migrating groundfish species. Inshore approaches to migrating *pelagic*

species, viz. capelin,[3] herring, mackerel, squid,[4] and pothead whale, on the other hand, have included use of inherited locations for stationary shore seines (for herring and capelin), and more mobile beach and bar seines for the same species; stationary traps (especially for squid); individual cast-nets; and community-wide drives, chiefly for pilot or 'pothead' whales.

The movements of pelagic species, more than of demersal, are felt to be affected by human interference or disturbance. There was therefore a general incentive favouring integration of extraction efforts above individual and extended-family levels. This incentive towards co-operative endeavour is especially apparent, for example, in the pothead whale fishery of Bonavista and Trinity Bays. It was impractical for the inshore fishermen of communities in these areas to attempt to capture the whales outside their local waters. Their boat and gear technology was unsuitable for such endeavour, and their quarry might be driven off or broken up and scattered prematurely. Long experience with the characteristics of their environment favoured driving them down long, narrow bays and on to stranding beaches. Once a pod of whales of a size deemed economic entered local waters demarked by headlands, right of access to them was usually restricted to any and all local fishermen willing to co-operate in their capture. Men from an adjacent community who happened to be in the area when the drive began could also participate and receive a full share. But a direct share of proceeds depended upon participation, and one had to be in the drive from the start (Mills 1971; Dean 1971; and cf. Williamson 1947).

What management ends underly these extractive strategies fitted to pelagic species? Maximisation of community access to seasonally fluctuating resources seems primary. There is no evidence of concern for husbanding a resource perceived as limited in absolute terms. Fishermen sought to extract as much as possible, and this was often less than they desired. Human limitations, technology, weather, access and movements of the quarry itself limited the extractive level. More would have been taken if it were possible.

Several conclusions may be drawn at this point: the successful articulation of small populations to the inshore fishing grounds of Newfoundland required development of primarily locally devised and shared boundary definition and control mechanisms. These are primarily concerned with rights to *access*. They limited competition and minimised conflict, and helped balance population (number of fishermen) against local resources, thereby avoiding resource division *ad infinitum* (Martin 1972). For pelagic species, they also minimised premature dispersal—an event with conflict potential. The management of access, viz. the very definition of access rights, their allocation, and continued attention to their maintenance and adequacy, served important socio-economic integrative functions. They bound community members together, and excluded others.

The Offshore Fishery

We now turn to the basic spatial management approaches encountered in the traditional offshore fishery of eastern Canada. Our specific reference is to the 'dory-fishing-schooner' regime based on the Northwest Atlantic codfish banks, and, to lesser degree, fishing grounds of the Gulf of St. Lawrence and Labrador coast.

This now extinct dory fishing or 'banking' schooner regime is poorly documented in comparison to inshore fishing adaptations in this same Atlantic region. There is little in detail for the period from about 1896, when Kipling's *Captains Courageous* appeared, to 1955, when the last banking schooner sailed from southern Newfoundland. Information from older fishermen who worked the Newfoundland, and Nova Scotian, 'bankers' leads us to conclude that Kipling's description of Gloucester banking schooner operations is for present purposes generalisable to eastern Canadian operations at large. Kipling's ethnography is frequently insightful and tempts lengthy reproduction, but we limit ourselves to the following findings.

First, banking schooner fishermen evidenced no concern that their predatory activity might alter the codfish population. Their skippers pursued the largest codfish, in part because bait and baiting-time were scarce, but no effort was made to husband the resource.[5] They sought to catch as much as possible in the shortest time until their salt was consumed. Vessel movements were linked with the twin aims of locating premium-size cod in optimal fishing densities. While the particulars of the fishing banks were general knowledge, premium-size, optimal density locations varied continuously. Banker skippers were nothing less than hunters; they shifted from ground to ground, endlessly dispersing and aggregating.

Second, their primary objectives being location and extraction, both matters fostered careful management of environmental-ecological knowledge and spacing mechanisms. In keeping with modern trawler operations on these grounds (see Andersen 1972), environmental–ecological information was unequally distributed among banker skippers—although this over-simplifies, there were those with the reputation of a 'master artist who knew the Banks blindfold' [*sic*] and could always find fish, and others who 'scrowged upon' these experts (Kipling 1961, pp. 39–40, 45, 71 and 80).

Striving to keep a good 'crowd' (crew) of dory fishermen from year to year, a skipper treated his knowledge, reputation and current information as scarce capital used to obtain exclusive, though temporary, predatory rights wherever possible. An appropriate complex of space-information management techniques developed about which little information is available (cf. Andersen 1972), as each skipper sought first rights to desired locations, and left others 'to bait big 'an catch small' (Kipling 1961; pp. 39–40).[6]

Keeping one's distance (dispersal) generally reduced risk and uncertainty in operations; especially important where navigational and other misunderstandings may have fatal consequences.[7] When capelin and cod concentrated, on the other hand, spacing was often reduced to oar's length at best, inspiring special risks and rules. Kipling vividly describes, for example, an estimated thousand fishermen in dories and schooners gathered one mile off the Virgin Rocks or eastern Shoals. Dense shoals of cod were visible in the shallow water,

> . . . swimming slowly in droves, biting steadily as they swam. Bank law strictly forbids more than one hook on one line[8] when the dories are on the Virgin or the Eastern Shoals; but so close lay the boats that even single hooks snarled . . . (1961, p. 102).

and tempers flared.

> Worse than any tangle of fishing-lines was the confusion of the dory-rodings below water. Each man had anchored where it seemed good to him, drifting and rowing round his fixed point. As the fish struck on less quickly, each man wanted to haul up and get to better ground; but every third man found himself intimately connected with some four or five neighbours. To cut another's roding is crime unspeakable on the Banks; yet it was done, and done without detection, three or four times that day (1961, p. 103).

A man caught doing so might be struck with an oar, knocked over his gunwale into the sea, to become the butt of amusement in slack times.

Thus maximisation of access holds the foreground in traditional (and modern) eastern Canadian offshore operations, as it did (and still does) inshore. Competition for access inspired a host of strategies, some still current in the modern, technologically advanced offshore fishery, where the advent of radio, radar and greater mobility, and vertically integrated *fleet* operations, have placed new stresses on the management of ecological information. There was no concern for resource depletion or overfishing for, after all, cod were conceived of as always moving about and never continually vulnerable to fishing effort. Territorially unbounded, they were there for the finding and taking. Finally, more than today, catch success could be treated as an important function of both skill *and* luck, rather than as evidence of absolute changes in the resource itself.

MODERN TRENDS: THE EFFECTS OF RESOURCE COMPETITION

Since the early 1950s, as a primary consequence of Confederation with Canada, the Newfoundland fishery has modernised and become more diversified technologically, and it now exploits an increasingly broader ecological spectrum. Despite these technological changes, gross production levels of the inshore and offshore fisheries have declined in recent years under increasingly intensified Canadian and foreign fishing effort. Moreover the total number of men employed in the inshore fishery increased steadily through the late 1950s and early 1960s—while the total output of this fishery actually *declined* (Copes 1969, p. 10).

For the most part, then, the trend towards awareness of an ecological crisis on the macro-level is not supported by parallel trends on the local-level. The new associations, and the general outcry of inshore fishermen against competition from the offshore fishery, have not yet embodied an appeal for personal restraint; rather, they have encouraged defensive and often somewhat aggressive postures on the part of inshore *and* offshore fishermen.

Yet the fact that resource-management has *not* appealed to fishermen on the level of personal cut-back of fishing effort need not be seen as an indication that no changes at all have occurred in the fisherman's orientation to his resource. Indeed, we feel that there are several important, if presently somewhat tentative, harbingers of change. The remainder of the paper is devoted to a brief consideration of three of these harbingers, all signifying the fisherman's increased awareness of *resource*, in addition to spatial, limitations.

First, it may be useful to designate the specific events which have precipitated such awareness at the local level. These are:

(1) Increased encroachment upon inshore fishing grounds;
(2) Outright failure in some traditional stocks;
(3) Advent of new government restrictions on fishing time and gear use.

1.   *Increasing Encroachment upon Inshore Fishing Grounds*

Encroachment by domestic and foreign draggers (trawlers) has received perhaps the greatest amount of publicity, and has certainly been the most salient evidence of pressure on his traditional resources for the inshore fisherman. Newfoundland and Labrador coastal fishermen have come accustomed to seeing large groups of draggers, many of foreign origin, fishing close to the 'shelf' (continental) and therefore within three miles of the coastline during the late winter and spring of each year. In both of these areas, draggers are able to continue operating in ice and wind conditions which smaller boats cannot tolerate, thus gaining a very real and visible advantage in resource-access over local boats. In addition, they often encroach spatially on the local boats' operations, sometimes actually sweeping-up nets, traps and long-lines, or simply crowding the inshoremen off the grounds.

Have these encroachments brought about an increased awareness of the pressure on total resources? Certainly, they are the major factor in the creation of SOFA, and a source of greatly increased pressure on local and regional fisheries authorities to step up enforcement of territorial limits and provide remuneration for loss of gear. The authors have encountered fishermen whose perception of the effects of dragger operations on local resources seem clear indeed; as one of these men commented, 'They's takin' the fish right out of our mouths, sir, and soon they'll be none left for anybody!' Yet the emphasis here is quite specifically on the depletion of the *local* resource, and the local fisherman's role is seen largely in spatial-competitive terms: an existing resource is being taken from those who have traditionally exploited it, and this calls for defensive action of some kind, associated with the need to retain privileged access.

There is nothing surprising about this, and there is certainly no reason to suppose that the pressure by dragger fleets would in itself lead to a development of local-level resource management. Fishermen view the depletion of local stocks, where it is readily apparent, in terms of decreasing personal income from fishing in the area; and so it is quite natural for fishermen to infer that a simple removal of draggers from the local area would not only reduce gear loss, but would also serve to restore stocks to their original levels.

The picture is somewhat less clear when we speak of confrontations between inshore fishermen and the migrant 'long-liner' operator. As explained below, long-liners are part of a technological progression within the inshore sector, and in many instances these boats and their associated catch technology are employed in a more or less traditional inshore adaptation; or, they are part of a gradual expansion of the scope of the inshore fishery. In the latter instance, an extended 'trip' pattern often emerges, with 'fleets' of long-liners (still fisherman-owned) from specific communities practising trips of a week or more to distant inshore (and occasionally offshore) grounds, and using local harbour facilities at the point of exploitation. The long-liner operators studied by Stiles (1972 a, b) on the Southwest coast are now engaged in such a pattern in connection with Danish-seining for greysole (witch flounder), as are a large number of operators from the island's northern bays who migrate annually to Port au Choix on the northwest coast for the summer and fall codfishery.

There are a number of cases from the eastern areas of the island where long-liner operators have begun to use traditional cod-trap berths of communities no longer regularly engaged in the inshore fishery. These latter occasions afford a particularly intriguing example of differential perception of resources by community-based fishermen, and indicate once again that the 'resource problem' is still largely understood in terms of spatial access.

In one such case, a group of particularly progressive long-liner-men from a Conception Bay community 'moved in' on a group of trap berths traditionally utilised by fishermen of an Avalon Peninsula community about 30 miles from the long-linermen's home. The fishermen of the latter community had failed to use these berths in recent years as wage-labour options in nearby St. John's became more attractive; and so, the encroachment by the long-linermen did not initially involve a direct confrontation of the two operations, but rather a single succession (the long-linermen were also employing traps).

Before long, however, the local fishermen, realising that their traditional trap-berths were being exploited on a regular basis by outsiders, moved to prevent this take-over. They appealed their case to the Department of Fisheries and won; thereafter, the long-linermen were compelled to use several marginal berths which were not traditionally employed by the local fishermen (i.e. not 'owned' by individuals or families), and were required to keep clear of the traditional berths, which were once again put to use by local fishermen.

The Department of Fisheries, in this case, ruled specifically that trap berths were locally owned and administered, and could not be used by outsiders to the community without express permission of the owners—which, notably was not forthcoming (Kent Martin, pers. communication); in effect, they reasserted and legitimised these traditional spatial management techniques. By the same token, however, the need for such legitimation was not apparent until the direct intervention by the long-linermen, and indeed the local fishermen's reaction was based in part on their recognition of resource limitations: they seem to have realised that even though the 'berths' were not put to use by these men, their use by others incurred a possible future loss of revenue. This was not, then, simply a case of privileged access to *space*, but also privileged access to an increasingly limited resource, and the fishermen acted to guarantee their use of this resource against *future* as well as present needs. It is true, of course, that this action did not entail a 'conservationist' strategy, but rather a personal *protectionist* one—yet some recognition of resource limitation was clearly in evidence.

Some of the more provocative and disruptive occurrences in recent years have been generated by several specialised fishing operations which have intruded regularly and directly into the inshore ecosystem. One, a rapidly expanded purse-seine fishery for herring, has involved operation of large boats, many of non-Newfoundland origin, in space traditionally inaccessible to all but the small-boat inshore fisherman. Herring seiners, equipped with sonar for navigating in shallow coastal waters, have been operating in several areas of Newfoundland for about four years now, capitalising on what was first thought to be a cyclic resurgence of the herring stocks of the area. For the first few years their operations were virtually unrestricted: no limitations of any sort were imposed on either technology, number of boats or total volume of catch—save, in the latter case, the limit imposed by plant processing capacity.

Because the seiners could operate in very shallow waters, their activities made it risky indeed for the small, inshore fisherman to put out nets or other gear in proximity to shore; those who did frequently lost them or experienced such extensive damage as to make further fishing appear unprofitable. Aside from their obvious and damaging intrusions on the inshore grounds, these seiners were also, it appears, depleting an important baitfish resource—although initially many scientists reasoned that intensive fishing would ameliorate the spectacular fluctuations to which herring has usually been susceptible (Templemann, 1966, pp. 90–1), hence in the long run stabilising the entire food chain, including those species (especially cod, but also haddock and redfish) traditionally caught by inshore fishermen.

Recent events indicate this may not be so, although the uncertainty introduced by seine operations has already pushed many marginal inshore fishermen into small-boat, herring gill-net operations of their own, selling the product as a high-cost, gourmet product. In some respects, this has been a defensive reaction on the part of local fishermen; driven from their inshore grounds by the seiner operations, the marginal operator has little alternative but to try the herring fishery himself. His ability to do this is guided by the lesser space requirements of herring gill-netting (vs. cod long-liners), and specifically by the availability of a few areas where the seiners cannot penetrate but where gill-nets may still be set. This reaction seems to be less a function of the inshore fishermen's own resource, than of spatial pressure on the traditional niche. On the other hand, since it is possible that depletion of herring stocks may already have led to a decrease in cod (the next link in the food chain), the behaviour of the inshoremen might also be seen as an attempt to diversify in the face of a possible failure of his principal resource.

2. Stock 'failures'

Certainly one of the clearest signals to the fisherman that changes in the resource may force changes in his exploitative pattern is the outright failure of some fisheries. There have in all probability been failures of some sort in the past, but as mentioned above these were seasonal or annual failures only; the fish always 'came back' again, reinforcing the fisherman's assumption that the changes were due to the characteristically erratic migratory behaviour of his resource. For example, the herring stock mentioned above has only been cyclically present on Newfoundland's west and south coasts (though it is usually considered a constant in discussion of the area's economic history; cf. e.g. Cheeseman *et al.* 1957; and Innis 1954). Templeman (1966, p. 91) reports that at least two large herring populations have 'largely disappeared' in the twentieth century, one in Fortune Bay and one in Labrador; both were the basis of elaborate seasonal fisheries, though in both cases the failures appear to have caused only a reallocation of manpower to other fisheries.

A more recent and spectacular failure, which could have long-lasting effects on the Newfoundland fisheries, was the sudden and apparently terminal depletion of the Labrador coastal cod stocks in 1970. Fishing 'on the Labrador' had long provided east-coast Newfoundland fishermen with a major source of their income as indicated earlier (see note 2). For a variety of practical economic reasons, and because of slight declines in the coastal stocks, this complex fishery gradually diminished in importance through the 1960s. The 'floaters', representing a somewhat larger capital investment, were the first to go; the 'stationars' remained, but their returns also dropped off and indeed the total number of 'stationars' declined significantly in the period.

By 1970 the fishery had reached a critical point, where a single bad year could render the situation hopeless. The 1970 season was precisely that: a *total* failure, for both floaters and stationars alike, and probably the last effective year for the Labrador operations. The reasons for this precipitate decline are not yet fully understood; explanations have ranged from fluctuations in some other component of the food-chain, to the more reasonable and locally credible tale that the 'draggers' or offshore boats had simply taken too much for too long. Indeed, dragger operations in the area had been extensive for several years previous to the failure, and some portions of the stock had undoubtedly been taken in the Gulf of St. Lawrence during the late winter and early spring.

Whatever the precise reason, the Labrador failure compelled a complete reassessment of the fishery on the east coast of the island, resulting in the solidification of a trend towards new boat-types, actually begun several years earlier. We have little information at present on these changes, though we would suggest that the changes in technology in the area (admittedly, not all due to the Labrador failure) do represent a trend towards decreased dependence on a single fishery or, more to the point, a single resource.

The east and south coasts of the island in particular are now the location of extensive 'long-liner' operations—a term referring to a new boat-type designed for a variety of inshore and 'nearshore' niches. 'Long-liners' are generally fisherman-owned, range in size from 35 feet to upwards of 75 feet, and may carry a variety of gear from long-lines to gill nets to Danish seines, depending on local conditions and product demand. They represent the major form of investment for fishermen moving out of the traditional inshore small-boat fishery, and they are in general a great deal more mobile than the inshore boats. There are at present no estimates available on the number of long-liners in operation in Newfoundland, but it is presumed that they number well over 1,000 units (cf. Goodlad, forthcoming).

If the growth of long-liner activity is at least partly a function of depleted or threatened inshore stocks, it is also a major factor in the continuing depletion of these stocks. Dean (1970) reports that long-liner operators have become highly mobile and competitive, ranging over large areas of the coast in pursuit of viable stocks. The 'competition' in this instance is for spatial access in areas where total fishing effort may have fallen off—as for example the traditional trap-fishermen mentioned before had temporarily abandoned their work for wage-labour, thus leaving their berths open to penetration by long-liner operators. Alternatively, some long-lines have encroached upon local grounds which are still being fully utilised. The local inshore fishermen have gradually become aware of their susceptibility to the long-liner invasion, and recognised the basic motive behind it: 'They cleaned out their own stocks and now they're going to do the same with what we have.' (Dean 1970, p. 10.)

It is of utmost importance to the individual long-liner operator, then, that he find new grounds in advance of other long-liners, thus capitalising on the possibly limited stock and also minimising the effects of resentment from local fishermen. The radio-telephone, a relatively new addition to the fisherman's technological kit in Newfoundland, increases his ability to locate such alternative grounds, because it facilitates contact with fishermen in other areas. When the intensity of fishing in a given area reaches intolerable levels, suggesting 'a reduction in total output, as well as the danger of one crew's gear becoming entangled with others' (Dean, 1970, p. 14), long-liner skippers may cast about for information on fishing returns elsewhere—radioing a friendly skipper in an adjacent bay, or simply 'listening-in' to their commentary on the day's activities, then moving into this area if the prospects are good.

That these long-liner fishermen are keenly aware of the effects of their activities on basic resources seems evident from their exceptional caution in providing catch-figures to other boats. Even where considerable space is available in an area, the thread of resource depletion looms large in fishermen's minds, and a radio 'hail' from an outsider will only rarely induce the fisherman to give detailed information of his good fortune. Aware of this reluctance, some operators prefer to call local fish plants directly, eliminating, as they see it, the problem of information distortion by bypassing those who have most to gain from it: 'Naturally, a fish plant manager wants all the fish resources he can possibly handle, and therefore would welcome a concentration of longliners within the general radius of his plant.' (Dean 1970, p. 15.)

Just how much the competitive mobility of long-liner operators can tell us of their perception of resource-limitation, is difficult to say from these data. Certainly, the rapid depletion of some local stocks is a major factor leading to this increased mobility; but the present writers' own research leads them to no definite conclusion as to whether these changes are viewed simply as *fluctuations*—i.e. as seasonal *movements* of a stock from one area to another or as *behavioural changes* in the stock—or whether the fisherman is adapting to the realisation that total stocks may be depleted by further intensification of effort. Stiles' research on long-liners operating in the Fortune Bay and St. George's Bay areas suggests that gradual depletion of their basic resource (grey sole) is very much apparent to the fishermen, and many realise that pressure on some areas has reached an acute phase. Symptomatic of this realisation are (*a*) a gradual return to more diversified fishing activities, following a brief burst of specialisation and (*b*) a tendency towards smaller crews, and concomitantly towards the elimination of seasonal or irregular crewmen in favour of a permanent 'core'. It should be noted that these are essentially economic responses: re-adjustments in the efficiency of the operation intended to increase or stabilise profits during periods of irregular returns. However, there are indications that the increasing scarcity of fish has brought more extensive behavioural changes, as well: e.g. many skippers, though reared in a relatively 'crowded' fishing environment, where tight spacing was normal, now view increasing concentrations of long-liners (even where spatial etiquette is maintained) as threatening, and move on to new grounds well before actual spatial encroachments occur.

3. *Government Restrictions*

It is in the application of actual government restrictions on fishing effort that we can see the clearest effects in terms of a changing orientation to resources on the part of fishermen. The greatest amount of data available concerns the salmon fishery, where restrictive measures of one sort or another have been applied by provincial and/or federal governments for well over a century, and where in the past few years the heightened international threat to this resource has prompted a whole new wave of such restrictions.

Throughout much of the island, salmon fishing is an important seasonal activity, carried out with anchored shore-nets and small boats; to date, the new limitations have had relatively little effect on these operations, save where specifications as to net size and mesh have been introduced, or licensing restrictions imposed. By contrast, on the south-west coast of the island, fishermen have been engaged for nearly forty years in the use of 'drift-nets' for salmon, employing large numbers of nets and a variety of boat sizes; and the impact of new restrictions has accordingly been much greater for these men than for salmon fishermen on the remainder of the island.

Since about 1960, the Department of Fisheries has imposed a succession of changes with regard to the maximum number of nets that can be employed by a single boat in the drift-net fishery, with several interesting results: First, the amount of space utilised by a single boat has decreased, though this has been of relatively little significance because of an initial increase in the number of units and because even at its height the density of units in this fishery was far less than for the cod fishery; and second, the marginal returns to labour fell to zero, as the basic capital input (nets) was now fixed permanently at a low level, inhibiting skippers from accepting new crewmen on a seasonal basis. The total number of participants in the fishery thus declined rapidly from 1960 on, and this tendency was accelerated when, in 1968, the government ruled that the number of permits for salmon fishing would be fixed at present levels, with no new licences to be issued at all. The suggestion that governments (or any external force) might be able to limit individual *access* to a resource (aside from limiting the means of exploiting it) was apparently novel for Newfoundland: it touched off a series of violent confrontations between fishermen and local Fisheries Department officers, in which the former sought to re-establish 'free access' while the latter, motivated by regulations based on international policy problems, cracked down stiffly in enforcing the new rule.[9]

The fisheries officers in fact had little local credibility, and their role was weaker still because of the abstract nature of the regulation: Canada's 'bargaining position' at ICNAF meetings was hardly sufficient cause, in the fishermen's eyes, for preventing a man from pursuing his life's work.

To the fisherman, the restrictions on amount and type of gear, and on the length of season itself, were far easier to accept than the refusal to issue additional licences. A large number of fishermen were caught off-base by this move, in most cases because they had failed to fish the previous year (hence bought no licence), or because they had left a boat in which only the owner held a licence and now wanted to fish on their own. While previous restrictions had affected all fishermen uniformly, then these new restrictions led to invidious distinctions; they were seen as exogenous limitations on *access* to the resource which gave some men a considerable economic advantage.

What does this bode for resource management? As we might expect, the fisherman's reaction in this instance was centred about the issue of access rights—*privileged space*; and his reaction was defensive, to wit: these are *my* resources, *my* living, and who are you to suggest that I cannot use them while my neighbour can? In the long run, however, these restrictions will undoubtedly have their intended effect: men are already turning away from the salmon fishery, although motivated in part by a devastating series of stock failures, and not by the restrictions *per se*. The intensity of conflict has been ameliorated, then—although it is important to note that the fishermen *never* accepted the right of the government to limit personal access, and have responded by circumventing the new regulations, rather than by adjusting to the need for a 'sustained yield'.

CONCLUSION

The foregoing examination of traditional approaches to marine resources and recent development effecting increased resource competition in Newfoundland fisheries has distinguished between resource and spatial management. It is apparent that Newfoundland fishermen, and fishery operators, remain primarily concerned with the establishment and maintenance of spatial-access privileges. Resource management is a relatively neglected dimension in their approach. It is equally clear that, regardless of this deficiency in local-level approach, the finite and endangered state of the marine biomass is an inescapable consideration; a harbinger of important transformations in the heretofore relatively unrestrained exploitation of Northwest Atlantic fishing grounds. Whether or not we project a future in which Canada and the United States assume exclusive exploitative–managerial rights to the Northwest Atlantic continental shelf, we must include in our projection some endpoint for unrestrained growth in the fisheries of this region—a Zero Fisheries Growth (ZFG) point. Controlled access and controlled extraction is in the offing. As social scientists, this anticipated state of affairs compels us to consider its shape and implications for the maritime peoples in this region.

What changes in cognition and values will occur among fishing people? May we expect independent fishermen, for example, to blithely accommodate themselves to increasingly rigorous restrictions of their operations? And what will this do to their commitment to fishing? Technological advancements in fishing operations are well along towards making it possible for the primary producers to 'harvest' rather than inefficiently hunt resources—yet the typical 'buccaneering' approach to fishing prevails. If such a harvesting approach is to materialise to full potential, what changes must occur on the operator-manager, and operator-fishermen levels? It will be necessary to develop mechanisms that bridge the co-operative boundaries of private interest. The shape of these mechanisms remain to be discerned, but we see no reason why existing organisations—e.g. fishermen's unions, co-operatives, lobbies—cannot be modified to accommodate them. Co-operative mechanisms and restraints bridging the boundaries of private interest or enterprise are suggested here.

Where once, therefore, fishermen could take as much as desired, given the opportunity, it is now imperative that they ask: 'How much am I entitled to?' There is no easy answer. It becomes a question of the kind of societies we wish to build, and what we discern to be our common ecological and human concerns. Weighing the marine biomass merely tells us how much we may take; not who should take it. The former is primarily a marine biological and oceanographic concern; the latter a social, economic and political one.

REFERENCES

1. We do not intend to suggest, of course, that fishermen lack any knowledge of the biological cycle or of the behaviour of particular resources; quite the contrary is true, as Morril (1967) and Forman

(1967) have demonstrated. However, their knowledge is probably less comprehensive and less systematically derived than is that of the marine biologist.

2. The Labrador 'floater' codfishery (see Black 1960) is best considered a distant water *inshore* operation. It involved the annual movement of schooners, equipped with from one to three trap fishing crews and necessary gear, from numerous east coast Newfoundland ports, to and from the Labrador coast. The 'floater' operations were complemented by a seasonal influx of 'stationars'—small-boat inshore operators from the east coast who took up residence in 'summer stations' on the coast. On arrival in June or July, in advance of the cod-run inshore, the 'stationars' were delivered directly to their destinations; the 'planters', the name given those who would operate from the schooner itself, congregated at the numerous seaward harbours from which they would operate each year. It seems likely that a draw for berths took place at the time of such congregations (*contra* Black 1960, p. 273). This allocative procedure probably followed an earlier period of somewhat unrestricted choice of berths in nearby waters, with consequent high risk.

3. For subsistence and bait, but also for crop fertiliser. 'When the capelin go down, it's no wonder the potatoes come up!'

4. Especially for fall bait, but also for subsistence and markets.

5. Portuguese dory fishermen—of the legendary 'White Fleet'—provide a minor variation on this theme: the dorymen are paid *by the fish*, and not by weight, hence prefer areas where the run of fish is small but dense.

6. 'Naturally, a man of Disko's reputation was closely watched—"scrowged upon" . . . by his neighbours, but he had a very pretty knack of giving them the slip through the curdling, glidy fogbanks.' (Kipling 1961, p. 80.)

7. ' . . . he (Disko, the skipper) objected to the mixed gatherings of a fleet of all nations. The bulk of them were mainly Gloucester boats, with a scattering from Provincetown, Harwich, Chatham and some of the Marine ports, but the crews drew from goodness knows where. Risk breeds recklessness, and when greed is added there are fine chances for every kind of accident in the crowded fleet, which, like a mob of sheep, is huddled round some unrecognized leader.' (Kipling 1961, p. 80.)

8. This was prior to regular use of long-lines on the Banks, and the 'line' referred to is a hand-line.

9. After several years of such conflict and uncertainty, the Canadian government decided—shortly after the initial draft of this paper was completed (April 1972)—to eliminate the salmon 'drift-net' fishery entirely. Those Newfoundland fishermen affected by this decision were awarded (and accepted) a series of yearly compensation payments, based on their earnings in the peak year of the fishery (1967); while at the time at which the final draft of this paper was completed (July 1972), several groups of New Brunswick fisherman—the only other drift-netters on the East Coast— were continuing to hold out against government offers of settlement.

Five · The Parameters of the Psychological Autonomy of Industrial Trawler Crews

JAN HORBULEWICZ

This paper considers the specific conditions of work in a deep-sea fishing vessel. It does not cover the differences between maritime and land professions since this has already been done in other papers.[1]

This paper is the result of a survey of life on board factory trawlers and will show the basic demands on the character of a crew member in a deep-sea fishing vessel.

In addition, it presents the results of research on the psychosocial effects on crews of prolonged stays at sea.

A fisherman's work takes place under a number of physical and psychosocial conditions which determine not only the specific nature of his occupation, but also the performance of his professional activities in difficult situations.

Difficult situations are those in which the execution of tasks (goals) requires an increased amount of physical and/or psychological force (motivation, knowledge, skill) compared with the average performance of other tasks because of various obstacles, difficulties, shortcomings, counteractions, pressures, threats or inhibitions. These factors may be physical or psychosocial.[2]

The term 'difficult situation' is relative. Whether a given situation is difficult or not is determined by the socio-economic standards of the community and the occupational group, as well as the level of development and the individual's level of experience. Certain types of difficult situations, such as overloads, inhibitions and threats, occur in the deep-sea fisherman's work.

The term 'overload' is applied to an excessive amount of matter-energy, information-handling or complicated tasks placed on a man. On fishing vessels, work is often done in extreme temperatures (e.g.

fishing during the fall–winter season in the North Atlantic, or in the tropics off West Africa); it also takes place in excessive noise, particularly on board the modern industrial trawlers.[3] Often the fisherman's occupation demands ten hours of work a day. His work and leisure are continuously influenced by changes in climatic and sea conditions.

Inhibition[4] is a physical or psycho-social state which prevents an individual from doing what he wants to do. On a deep-sea ship inhibition takes the form of limited personal space, limited freedom of movement, limited choice of society and leisure activity, and most of all of separation from family and closest friends. Inhibitions also take the form of normative acts (rules, orders, prohibitions) which control life on board in an almost military manner. Biophysical forces affecting the ship, e.g. storm, or the lack of fish on fishing-grounds, should also be noted as factors contributing to states of inhibition.

Threat is increased probability of loss of a man's most valued properties. The fisherman's work is persistently accompanied by threats. This is not due solely to the fact that shipping still involves certain risks to life; the compactness of accommodation; the large amount of gear, equipment and men in a relatively small and unstable space poses the threat of injury. Previous research from 1965 to 1967 shows that 36 out of every 1,000 fishermen on the factory trawlers belonging to 'DALMOR', the largest deep-sea fishing enterprise in Poland, were affected by injuries.[6] It should also be noted that cyclical marital separation constitutes a certain threat to the emotional link between the fisherman and his wife. All this contributes to the term 'personal threat'.

All the difficult situations occurring on board a deep-sea fishing vessel have not been mentioned but the principal types have been noted. Some of these difficult situations also occur in other professions. The specific nature of seafaring however, consists in such situations appearing together and cyclically. Difficult situations have certain consequences for a man's organism and personality. These consequences are deprivations.

Deprivation is a temporary withdrawal of values which are indispensable to his well-being and/or the efficiency of his organism and/ or his personality. In other words, by deprivation a man has been deprived of the possibility of satisfying a certain need for a shorter or longer period.

Deep sea fishing interferes with the needs for relaxation, sexual gratification and for emotional contact, for security, and for personal interests and inclinations. Are all these types of deprivation equally aggravating or is any one of them particularly stressful? It is commonly accepted that the 'neutral' or 'harmless' length of deprivation varies according to the type of the affected need. A man can normally function in a deprived situation for only a certain defined time. In respect of biological needs such as hunger, thirst, the time of deprivation which does not cause changes in the organism and in the man's behaviour is—as we know—relatively very short. For some psychosocial needs the 'neutral' time of deprivation is much longer. But does this mean that the hierarchy of the importance of satisfying various needs is stable and definitely established? Several facts indicate that this is not the case.

As reports of people who passed through German concentration camps prove,[7] chronic malnutrition led to 'dreams of food [which] took almost all the consciousness' of the prisoners. Reports of frontline soldiers show that after several sleepless nights during fighting their principal desire was to lie down in any convenient place, even in a roadside ditch, and sleep; the deadly danger they were exposed to diminished under the influence of the overwhelming need to sleep. Similarly, persons isolated from their social milieux wish to return to it after an absence of a few weeks.

These and similar findings show that the intensity of stress from the deprivation of given needs is a function not only of the type of need, but also the duration and degree of that deprivation. Thus the importance of the satisfaction of each of the needs, in relation to other needs, varies. This means that a man shows a varying independence in time from external alienation in respect of various needs. The longer an individual remains in the extraneutral time of deprivation, the more important and subjectively more annoying becomes the need.

As far as the need for optimal stimulation is concerned, fishermen and seamen are only partially deprived. Excessive noise or vibration occurs only in certain parts of the ship (e.g. engine room, industrial department) and the workers are exposed to these factors mainly when on duty. Low or high temperatures are also only of short duration. Technical advancement in safety and hygiene at work (e.g. air-conditioning, control-rooms, etc.) have reduced physical discomfort. Safety has been improved through increased stability of the ship's hull, increased engine output, perfection of navigational devices and the mechanisation and automation of difficult tasks.

But the fisherman's relaxation is considerably decreased when the catches are good on the fishing grounds. Some groups of fishermen work 18 and more hours per day.[8] However, the catch is not always so good that it causes a disturbance in established work and leisure cycles and there are periods of relative idleness not only en route to or returning from the grounds, but also when 'looking for fish'. At these times the fisherman's personal inclinations and interests can be pursued. On board modern ships there are libraries and club rooms with games, movies are shown and do-it-yourself facilities and photo laboratories, are available.

But there is a group of seafarers' needs which are not met when at sea. These are the needs related to family and marital life. The performance of his job requires the deep-sea fisherman (or seaman) to stay aboard his ship far from home, family and friends, over prolonged, cyclically repeated periods and it is suggested that this kind of deprivation is the most important factor in reducing his job-effectiveness.

In order to check this assumption a questionnaire was administered to deep-sea fishermen and seamen to enquire into the most aggravating factors in their work. They were asked to point out the three most important of nine stressors:

(1) limited space to move,
(2) technical working conditions/noise, vibration, etc.,
(3) hydrometeorological and climatic conditions,
(4) work organisation on board,
(5) work organisation in home port,
(6) personal relations on board,
(7) relationship to owners,
(8) separation from family and friends/family, wife, fiancée, etc.,
(9) work remuneration system.

Answers were received from 217 fishermen and 172 seamen. 84 per cent of the former and some 59 per cent of the latter mentioned the eighth factor (separation from family and friends) as the major emotional stressor. This striking difference between both groups can be explained by the fact that some of the seamen sailed on shorter lines and therefore visited their homes more frequently than the deep-sea fishermen. That separation from family and friends constitutes the main stress creating factor in deep-sea fishermen's work has also been confirmed by subsequent research in which the set of values of this group was determined. The subjects were required to place, in order, eleven different values such as 'position in duty hierarchy', 'money', 'consistent crew', 'emotional bonds to family', etc. The value most appreciated, most important in life, had to be mentioned first, the least precious, last. Responses were received from 313 fishermen.

Generally, intragroup differences of opinions were considerable. There was, however, considerable agreement about one value. More than 83 per cent of respondents ranked 'emotional bonds to family' in the first (64.9 per cent) or second place (18.5 per cent). As we see, the results conform astonishingly with the previous findings. Thus we have to admit that family is highest in value for most fishermen. It should be added that the second most important ranking (43.4 per cent) response was 'pay'. This indicates the important role of economic motivation in fishermen's work.

The placing of family bonds first is not exclusively a Polish phenomenon. Research by French sociologists showed that French seamen and fishermen regarded their occupation as inferior to professions ashore, mainly because of the deprivation of normal family life.[9] Previously, this lack was compensated for by a considerable difference in income, to the advantage of seafarers. These differences have declined rapidly during recent years following economic progress ashore, and a decrease in the yield of traditional fishing grounds.

Antarctic researchers—Byrd, Bombard, Slocum, etc.—stressed that the greatest threat to their survival was not the risks of the peculiar environment, but their solitude and the surrounding monotony. Rear-Admiral Richard E. Byrd, while at an Antarctic outpost, wrote the following words: '. . . it appears that I cannot bear my solitude indifferently—it is too great'.[10]

It is well known that the environment of the submarine is crowded. One should expect therefore the tightness of space to be an important psychological problem for the crew. It appears, however, that the majority of seamen adapt perfectly to such conditions. King and Weybrew report that only 20 per cent of 331 individuals pointed to 'imprisonment' as a negative aspect of life in a submarine. Weybrew finds that officers in command of submarines reported only 7 per cent of crewmen as having been disqualified after six months of service at sea because of 'extreme disgust at crowded conditions'.[12] Whereas, a serious stress form is preoccupation with family, or anxiety about his wife, as the seaman has no influence on their fate and exchange of information is insufficient.[13] These few examples support the conclusion of Margaret Lantis who, discussing the research results of various writers (Chance, Gundersen, Vallee, *et al.*) dealing with the influence of environmental stresses on the behaviour of natives in Polar regions of Canada, Alaska and Norway, stated that '. . . important environmental stresses derive today rather from social environment than from physical because technology improves the effect of climate and other physical factors'; and further '. . . the physical environment should be considered in respect of its indirect rather than direct effects'.[14] Lantis draws attention to the fact that the many stresses mentioned in various research papers have one common element: the loss of autonomy. Among other things, this consists of the loss of social support from the individual's family, forced separation from home, as well as the involved loss of the family autonomy.

It seems that the principal obstacle to adaptation in the previous cases was presented not by the individual's removal from his normal environment (home, country, own community) and location (isolated) in an unusual environment, but rather simply by separation from his family and friends. The seamen's wives have to face similar difficulties in bearing their 'loneliness'. Many of them experience a particular psychological crisis each time they are separated from their husbands. C. A. Pearlman differentiates three phrases in this crisis: protest, distress, indifference. He writes: 'Experience of the majority of seamen's wives indicates that the real adaptation to the crisis caused by separation requires the capacity to be alone.'[15] (Pearlman conducted research into the life-patterns of wives of nuclear submarine crewmen.) It seems the origin of this capacity is to be sought in early childhood when the little child develops a feeling of security based on experienced help and support received from the nearest persons (usually the mother) in moments of weakness.[16]

Summarising what has been said so far, the following should be stated:

(1) Work in deep-sea fisheries and sea-transport takes place in conditions of stress;
(2) The principal stressor is the social-emotional separation from one's closest persons;
(3) This separation causes:
   deprivation of emotional contact needs (e.g. separation from wife, children, family, fiancée, etc.),

reduced communication with family (deprivation of information),

deprivation of socio-emotional support from family in the isolated psychosocial ship-community (loss of family autonomy).

The larger number of fishing fleets and an improvement in fishing technology in recent years has resulted in a decline in the biological efficiency of fishing grounds in the Baltic Sea, the North Sea and the North Atlantic. Operational costs have risen in tandem with the modernisation of fishing vessels. Economic causes therefore force deep-sea fishing enterprises to send their vessels and crews on ever longer cruises. While the augmentation of the vessel's range is determined by economic efficiency—processes depending on administrative decisions, the longer time spent by crews at sea, the worse their general conditions of work will be and the effect on health and motivation to work.

First, there may be an increase in psychological disorders, especially psychoneuroses and psychosomatic illnesses.[17] Secondly, there may be a decline in workers willing to go to sea and in recruitment. In the 1960s in Western Europe there was a massive decline in the number of fishermen. In France alone the number dropped to 8,000 between 1961 and 1969. Similar declines in West Germany and the Netherlands were reported. An explicit distaste for the profession of fisherman was discovered among the youth of these countries.[18]

Assuming an increase in living standards for shore workers in European countries in the next few years, a further decline in the attraction of seafaring (fisherman and seaman) is to be expected. As already said, work in deep-sea fishing precludes, to a greater or lesser degree, the satisfaction of certain human needs. When deprived a man can function normally for only a certain time, this period differing for various needs. In this, independence from external sources (autonomy) varies. Since work at sea mainly causes deprivation of psychosocial needs, the determination of the optimal duration of a voyage consists primarily in discovering what the potential psychological autonomy of fishing crews may be. By psychological autonomy we mean that specific factor in a man's personality which allows him to perform his task within a given time without lowering his functional level as a worker and group member although he is in a deprived state. This characteristic is measured by the time of deprivation recorded before a decrease in functional level becomes apparent. It must be remembered that, because the seafarer is a human being, this sort of investigation is necessarily imprecise and varies from man to man.

It is possible, therefore, only to define that specific period of time when psychological deterioration threatens the crewman's health and lowers his efficiency (reliability). The first exhaustion of psychological autonomy occurs with the appearance of:

(a) considerable decrease in motivation to work;
(b) deterioration in orientation and increase in faulty activity (leading to production faults, breakdowns and accidents);
(c) worse personal relations (violation of discipline, conflicts, quarrels).

Because of individual variations, one should speak not of psychological autonomy in general, but of individual psychological autonomy (IPA). Thus, attempts to determine the limits of fishing crews' autonomy at sea can lead only to the determination of the autonomy most frequently encountered. A state of deprivation may lead to an increase in stress, emotional alertness and aggressive actions (destruction of things and hostile attacks on people). Aggressive actions usually reduce the extent of strain.[19]

It appears from other psychological research that emotional alertness results in poorer perceptual, intellectual and psychomotional activity.[20] If the emotional strain caused by the state of deprivation is of a long-term, chronic nature, fatigue symptoms,[21] such as errors in work and decrease in a man's co-ordinative and integrative aptitude[22] may also emerge. In other words, prolonged work at sea constitutes a threat to a man's reliability.

Whether this is a potential state only, or results in a real decrease in efficiency poses the principal question to which we are striving to find an answer in our research. More precisely—how long can a man endure the uninterrupted influence of these various depriving factors without lowering his psychological and psychomotional efficiency? We should first examine the research methods used and then the findings.

The principal task was the measurement of psychological attitude dynamics and personal interaction dynamics of fishing crews. Therefore, indicators of these attitudes had to be developed. For the purpose of our research, we adopted a *barometer of emotional tension* to measure indicators related to the seafarer's *emotional state*, *thinking efficiency, psychomotional efficiency* and *personal interaction.* This is Janet Taylor's *Manifest Anxiety Scale* (MAS) adapted for our own use. Furthermore, the *Maudsley Personality Inventory* (MPI) and *Eysenck Personality Inventory* (EPI) have been applied to determine the *emotional state. Thinking efficiency* has been determined by *Dobruszek's test* (DOD) which consists in adding and subtracting two-digit numbers within a given time. The *psychomotional efficiency* (precision of movements and response time of choice) has been examined with the aid of a Polish-made *tremometer* and a Belgian-made *Bettendorff's Reactionmeter.* The results of psychological research have then been supplemented by data concerning accidents and disciplinary infringements as a function of voyage duration.

A group of 61 fishermen underwent examination four times at intervals of about 40 days spread over the duration of their stay at sea by employing the *Emotional Tension Barometer* (ETB).

Table 5.1 shows mean rates in units of the 82-points scale and of the percentage scale. As the table shows, the state of *emotional tension* (ET) of the fishermen increases gradually in proportion to the length of their stay at sea. The ET level increased by 6.4 per cent between day 5 and day 125 of the cruise. This increase proved statistically to be highly significant ($p > 0.001$), and the difference between the tests carried out on day 5 and day 85 was also significant. The fastest increase of ET, however, appeared between day 85 and day 125 of the voyage. These data indicate that crew members at this stage of the voyage more frequently suffered such states as difficulty in concentrating, mobile anxiety (difficulty in sitting still), nightmares, excitement leading to insomnia, high susceptibility, feeling of nervous exhaustion and tension, homesickness, lack of job satisfaction, and physiological disturbances such as stomach troubles, perspiring at low temperatures and headaches. Apart from the statistical evidence of emotional tension, Table 1 also shows *standard deviation* (sd). But the individual measures showed great differences in the ET level of different persons.

Accurate analysis enabled the exposition of four sub-groups showing different directions of variation of measured variables:

systematic increase of ET level in subsequent tests, decrease of tension in second and third tests, and increase in fourth test, increase of tension in second and third tests, and decrease in fourth test.

TABLE 5.1 *Increase of emotional tension level (ET) of fishermen throughout duration of cruise.*

Measure no. (a)	Stay at sea (days) (b)	Size of group (c)	Level of tension			Test of differences	
			82 p. scale		percentage scale (f)		
			x (d)	s.d. (e)		u (g)	p (h)
1	5	50	25.8	21.3	31.5	u 1 × 2 = 1.87	<0.05
2	45	91	26.7	19.8	32.5	u 2 × 3 = 1.87	<0.05
3	85	91	27.9	17.8	34.0	u 1 × 3 = 2.70	>0.01
4	125	41	31.1	18.1	37.9	u 3 × 4 = 4.05	>0.001

Only 5 per cent of the individuals showed a constant level of emotional tension in all tests.

These findings lead to the important conclusion that the increase in ET level depends not only on the duration of stay at sea, but simultaneously reminds us of the higher tension level of most subjects after approximately 85 days than after 5 days at sea. These conclusions were confirmed in a study of emotionally imbalanced state dynamics of the sample of 130 fishermen examined on the 15th, 55th, 95th and 135th days of the voyage. Thus, the differentiation of subsequent test results variation was so great that we could extract five sub-groups with significant differences in *emotional imbalance* (EI) dynamics by means of variance analysis. The results of the examination of these five sub-groups are shown in Table 5.2.

Worthy of consideration are two sub-groups, B and C; with particularly large populations (30.8 per cent and 26.2 per cent of total subjects respectively), showing opposite directions of result variation. In sub-group B imbalance rose gradually nearing the pathological limit approximately by the 95th day, while sub-group C began the cruise with an EI level near that which the former sub-group reached at the end of cruise. However, towards the end of the cruise sub-group C became more stable emotionally.

The next two sub-groups (D) and E (representing together 28.4 per cent of the total population studies) show skewed EI dynamics curves: decrease and rise, and rise and decline. Only 14.6 per cent of the subjects had a state of emotional imbalance more or less constant in all four examinations. Thus, certain states such as change of mood and humour, feelings of depression without any obvious reason, nervousness and sleeplessness show high and multi-directional dynamics. A clear increase of EI over the duration of the cruise was shown by 31 per cent crew members.

None of the sub-groups passed the pathological limit estimated at 66 per cent. This is, of course, a mean figure and does not mean that there were no individuals who developed symptoms of psychoneurotic disturbances. The percentage of persons with clearly developed neurosis symptoms discovered in four subsequent examinations amounted to 17.3 per cent, 15.6 per cent, 13.4 per cent and 18.4 per cent. It appears that symptoms of pathological emotional imbalance emerge mostly at the beginning and at the end of the cruise, and are somewhat more pronounced in the latter case.

So it appears that level of emotional tension and degree of imbalance are not only a function of time at sea but depend also on

TABLE 5.2   *Imbalance dynamics of fishermen working at sea, in five subgroups. N = 130.*

Subgroup (a)	State (in per cent scale) during stay at sea					Test u (f)	$p*$ (g)
	15 days (b)	55 days (c)	95 days (d)	135 days (e)		
A $N = 19$	36.4	37.5	35.5	35.4	$b \times c = 3.51$	<0.001
B $N = 40$	41.7	49.8	62.5	59.9	$c \times d = 5.48$	>0.001
					$b \times c = 5.83$	>0.001
C $N = 34$	61.5	47.4	40.4	33.5	$c \times d = 2.91$	>0.01
					$d \times c = 2.77$	>0.01
D $N = 18$	49.2	30.8	33.9	64.2	$b \times c = 6.03$	>0.001
E $N = 19$	34.2	50.9	33.7	18.8	$b \times c = 5.52$	>0.001

* p values given only for differences significant at the 0.05 level at least.

other factors. Among other things, circumstances of home port visits have also to be considered.

We know from frustration theory that deprivation leads to aggressive behaviour. We should expect therefore that at sea acts of aggressive behaviour become more frequent in proportion to the length of the voyage. Data about fights on ships was therefore collected. The data covered five years of entries in the official log books of deep-sea fishing vessels belonging to one Polish owner. The data, in chronological order, is given in Table 5.3.

TABLE 5.3 *Increase of aggressiveness (according to fight rates) of fishing crew members as function of time at sea.*

Measure no.	Time of crew at sea (days)	Mean rate of fights per 100 cruises
1	1–30	3.0
2	31–60	3.4
3	61–90	5.0
4	91–120	9.5

As we see, the mean rate of fights per 100 cruises increases clearly after the 60th day at sea. Between the 90th and 120th day it is three times greater, compared with the first or second month at sea.

Not all cases of aggression are entered into the ships' log books; only the most serious ones are recorded. The sort of injuries found were black eyes, cut heads, broken jaws, concussion, cracked skulls, first and second degree burns to the face. This proves that after the crew has been at sea for ninety days there is a considerable worsening of personal interactions. We know from other sources that during prolonged cruises acts of aggression against objects also occur, e.g. breaking glasses, deliberate destruction of tools or equipment, etc.

The next aspect of the seafarer's life to be analysed is the effect of the duration of a voyage on *thinking efficiency*. The rate of counting (addition and substraction) per time unit was used as an indicator of thinking efficiency. This was performed eight times in twenty-day intervals on 81 subjects. Table 5.4 shows mean percentage errors made by the crew members in the tests.

The table shows neither stability, nor any defined trend. Two decreases of efficiency are clearly marked: around the 75th and 155th day of cruise. However, there was such variation that we selected

TABLE 5.4 *Fishermen's counting efficiency in relation to numbers of days spent at sea.*

Measure no. (a)	Time at sea (days) (b)	Per cent of errors (c)	Level of difference significance (u-test) (d)
1	15	7.9	
2	35	7.4	
3	55	7.3	$u\ 1 \times 4 = 2.93\ p\ 0.01$
4	75	8.9	$u\ 3 \times 4 = 2.62\ p\ 0.01$
5	95	7.2	$u\ 4 \times 5 = 3.54\ p\ 0.001$
6	115	7.4	
7	135	7.3	$u\ 7 \times 8 = 1.96\ p\ 0.05$
8	135	8.6	

four subgroups which showed different performance levels. The results of the further examination of these subgroups are presented in Table 5.5. Only six subjects (7.3 per cent of the sample) demonstrated relatively insignificant variations in thinking efficiency whereas performance level was relatively high in all examinations (sub-group A).

Thirty-four subjects (i.e. 42 per cent of total) showed a decrease and subsequent increase in efficiency. The lowest level of performance occurred around the 75th day of the cruise (sub-group D). In twenty-one subjects (25.9 per cent) the opposite result was shown: first increase then decrease. The lowest level of performance occurred on the 155th day (sub-group E). Twenty persons (24.7 per cent) showed a temporary variation of efficiency and the lowest performance level occurred roughly on the 15th day (sub-group F). Thus the majority of crew members studied showed a clear breakdown in thinking efficiency after a longer period at sea: 75 or 155 days. However, efficiency dynamics in various sub-groups prove that decrease in performance level is not just a function of time spent at sea.

We tested psychomotional efficiency on the same group using a tremometer to determine the position of final movements on the 220 mm scale. Considering the mean output of the whole group examined, it appeared that the control of movements become somewhat worse after thirty-five days at sea. However, once again there was a great deal of individual variation.

TABLE 5.5 *Counting efficiency of fishermen during work at sea, in four sub-groups.* $N = 81$

Measure no. (a)	Day of cruise (b)	Per cent of tasks correctly performed in sub-groups			
		A $N = 6$ (c)	D $N = 34$ (d)	E $N = 21$ (e)	F $N = 20$ (f)
1	15	96.3	93.9	90.81	88.7
2	35	96.1	91.4	93.0	93.2
3	55	95.9	90.4	95.4	92.8
4	75	97.7	88.1	94.8	89.9
5	95	95.2	91.4	94.9	92.8
6	115	96.9	91.3	94.4	93.1
7	135	96.9	93.1	91.3	91.4
8	155	96.4	93.0	84.6	91.5

Note: Significant differences of measures appeared to be:
(1) in sub-group D: (2) in sub-group E:

1 and $22u = 7.83\ p > 0.001$ 1 and $3u = 4.75\ p > 0.001$
4 and $7u = 5.87\ p > 0.001$ 6 and $7u = 6.81\ p > 0.001$

(3) in sub-group F:
1 and $2u = 3.87\ p > 0.001$
2 and $4u = 2.95\ p > 0.01$
4 and $6u = 2.84\ p > 0.01$

The lowest mean efficiency of sight-motion co-ordination was found as follows:

for 47 per cent of subjects between the 75th and 95th day;
for 42 per cent between the 15th and 55th, and between the 115th and 135th day;
for 11 per cent—on the 15th, and between the 95th and 115th day of work at sea.

It appears from these figures that the efficiency of movement control is related not only to working time at sea, though most fishermen had a decrease in efficiency after approximately seventy-five days at sea. For the purpose of obtaining an additional indicator of psychomotional efficiency, the reaction time of choice (alternatives) in two crews of 74 and 64 members respectively was tested. The reaction time after 100 days at sea appeared to be 10 per cent longer than that obtained in tests on the fiftieth day at sea. This difference proved to be statistically significant above the 96 per cent probability level.

Thus the speed of response in complex situations (alternatives) worsened considerably after 100 days at sea.

Finally we must look at the effect of length of voyage on the frequency of accidents. As a rule, the psychological state of the worker, his psychomotional efficiency, is the immediate cause of the accident. Therefore accident dynamics may be one of the indicators of workers' efficiency. Table 5.6 shows a mean distribution of accidents, in time

TABLE 5.6 *Distribution of accidents during the cruise*

Item no.	Time at sea (days)	Mean rate of accidents per 100 cruises
1	1–20	37.1
2	21–40	32.4
3	41–60	35.1
4	61–80	45.0
5	81–100	28.5
6	101–120	19.9

order, per 100 cruises. A striking factor is the finding that most of the accidents occurred between the 60th and 80th day of cruises.

These findings coincide strikingly with the psychological data referred to above.

GENERAL CONCLUSIONS

In general, a long voyage is detrimental to a fisherman's psychological well-being leading to a loss in his economic and personal efficiency.

Secondly, the relationship of this deterioration to the duration of the voyage is complex, and does not show linear relationship, but is rather of a cyclic nature.

Thirdly there is individual resistance to the unfavourable influence of long-term stays at sea. This is shown by:

(*a*) The differing degrees of psychological disturbance and the

(*b*) different times disturbance shows itself—a reflection of individual psychological autonomy.

Fourthly, in our study the first 'critical' phase occurred most frequently between the 70th and 90th day of work at sea.

Fifthly, the exhaustion of individual autonomy does not signify a complete exhaustion of a man's psychological capacity, but a significant temporary decline in his function both as worker and crew member. In addition, the results show that disturbances were not only a function of time passed at sea, but also of other factors.

Finally, further tests need to be carried out to establish precisely what the determinants of psychological disturbance in crew members are and what resistance each individual has to shipboard stresses. These findings would establish the right length of voyage and the right choice of crew for the optimum prosecution of deep sea fishing.

REFERENCES

1. See for example: V. Aubert and O. Arner (1958–9); O. Arner (1961); V. Aubert and O. Arner (1962); K. Weibust (1958).
2. On the subject of difficult situations, see W. Tomaszewski, *Introduction to Psychology;* Warsaw, P.W.N., 1963.
3. The noise levels on board a modern diesel-electric trawler are in the 50–105 dB. range.
4. 'Inhibition' is used interchangeably with the related terms of 'blockage', 'hampering' and 'counteraction'.
5. Lloyd's Register for 1965, 1966 and 1967 show that 154, 159 and 163 ships, respectively, were lost at sea.
6. J. Horbulewicz (1968).
7. P. Chodoff (1970), p. 79.
8. Note D. Gerst (1968); J. Tunstall (1961); K. Weibust (1958).
9. R. Benjamin (1970).
10. N. M. Burns and D. Kimura (1963), p. 168.
11. Ibid.
12. B. B. Weybrew (1963), p. 93.
13. J. H. Earls (1969).
14. M. Lantis (1968), p. 578.
15. C. A. Pearlman (1970), p. 947.
16. J. Bowalby (1963).

17. J. Horbulewicz (1970 *a*); J. Horbulewicz (1970 *b*).
18. For a discussion of this point see R. Benjamin (1970); D. Gerst (1968) and J. Horbulewicz (1972).
19. J. Reykowski (1968) op. cit., pp. 245–6.
20. See for example, L. Postman and J. S. Bruner (1948); G. S. Reynolds (1960); R. S. Lazarus, J. Deese and R. Hamilton (1954).
21. W. Missiuro (1947).
22. H. Schmidtke (1965).

Six · A Possible Perspective on Deprivations

BRYAN NOLAN

This short exploratory paper is concerned with a theoretical approach to certain aspects of seafaring life. It is in three parts: the first looks at sociological models in general and tries to stress the status of a model as a nominal construct, a thing to be invented to aid analysis of social actions. In the second part a brief outline sketch is given of a possible total institution model of a ship, and lastly some deprivations suggested by the model are touched on.

As Alvin Gouldner has said,[1] with every idea or intellectual package come certain sentiments and feelings. This seems to be no less true for total institution models than it is for Weberian bureaucracies. He refers to these orientations that theories suggest or generate as the 'Metaphysical Pathos of Ideas' and there seems little doubt that in the case of a total institution perspective the emphasis does tend to be on the dark, pessimistic and restrictive side of seafaring. A construct which has such implications and undertones is unlikely to find much favour with interests concerned with the recruitment, employment or training of seamen, or those who see it as a distasteful and oblique attack on some of the more romantic aspects of seafaring. I appreciate their feelings, but this does not detract from the sociological usefulness or epistemological value of the construct and I hardly need to say to those here today that seafaring does have other more positive, beneficent and enjoyable aspects. The importance of a total institution model is that it focuses attention on intraorganisational factors, especially power, which I take to be a key sociological variable in looking at social interaction aboard merchant ships.

This will be mainly a theoretical discussion deriving from a specific kind of sociological model—that of the ship as a total institution. As these tentative and theoretical perspectives stem from a particular kind of model, we should first examine sociological models in general and then look briefly at some possible elements of a total institution model before saying something about some possible sources of deprivation at sea that are suggested by the use of such a model.

A model is an abstract human construct which attempts to structure and give meaning to particular social situations or recurring social patterns of action. As such, a model is not necessarily intended to be descriptive of any part of the 'real' social world. Neither is it intended to be prescriptive or condemnatory. It is an articulated concept, not of how it is, or how it should be, but a suggestion for one type of partial interpretation of 'social reality' as experienced by social actors in the situation.

As Braithwaite[2] mentions, a model is not a model 'of' something, it is a model 'for' some purpose. Its purpose is to give us a new and possibly greater sociological understanding of phenomena. But to talk of sociological understanding or meaningfulness is to beg even bigger questions and raise major controversies.

It is no obvious criticism to say that a model does not describe shipboard 'reality'; many of the most fruitful models in the history of science have in fact been gross violations of the common sense and what passed for conventional wisdom at the time. Any one model is neither true nor untrue, but just more or less useful. The way it is useful is in enabling us to see familiar things—in our case social phenomena—in novel and suggestive ways. We need to ask: Can it inform our thinking in a sociologically useful way and suggest new ways to structure, interpret and give coherence and meaning to well-known patterns of social action?

According to this kind of view, sociological structure is imposed on the material by the model. That is to say we do not 'discover' social structure in situations, we impress a pattern and a meaning on it according to our perspective. Meaning is not discovered in social situations, it is given to them. Knowledge in this sense is a human artefact or construct and something to be invented rather than discovered.

If we take this view, it would follow that there is no one 'correct' or right model but just ones that may be more or less appropriate to our understanding of the task in hand—but of course part of what we see as the task in hand or problems arising from a situation is also to some extent a result of our initial perspective. Each model or conception we use for ordering phenomena affects not only our perceptions and observations but also impresses a certain shape to our findings and conclusions as well as shaping our view of initial 'problems'. In this sense at least no model or conceptual language can ever be value free. Each brings with it acknowledged or latent sentiments and preferences. Using a nautical idiom, in the same way that every chart or representation used in navigation implies a perspective and a distinctive method of viewing, so each and every model, calculus, language or description of 'reality' must be made from some specific standpoint and so contain explicit or implicit assumptions which structure perceptions, problems and conclusions.

This is to say that each model being only a partial perspective on social actions, emphasises certain areas and obscures others. With each model certain factors are stressed (and herein lies at least the potential danger of reification) and others omitted from full consideration or obscured. For instance, if the strength of a total institution model does lie in its close examination of intra-organisational determinants or sources of action here also lies its major weakness, the fact that it takes little account of extra-organisational factors. Each perspective has not only advantages but opportunity costs as well. Every choice logically implies an exclusion, every liberation means some constraint. The power to liberate thought from conventional modalities is always conditional.

We may draw analogies from two areas of study, geometry and celestial mechanics.

If one required to survey a small area of coastline one could do so using either Euclidean geometry or a non-Euclidean system, such as spherical geometry. Neither model would give a totally accurate description of the area, but both could be made to give the degree of accuracy required. Neither model is true or false but just more or less useful in arriving at an interpretation or way of looking at a small area of the earth.

Similarly, both the Copernican and Ptolemaic systems or models of looking at the solar system can, with small modifications, be made to yield comparable predictions of the positions of planetary bodies. However, accuracy of position prediction might only be one criterion in deciding which model might be the more suitable for a given purpose; Ptolemy's cycles and epi-cycles are much more cumbersome and unwieldy than the elegant solar-centred circular orbits of the Polish monk. With religious considerations laid aside, principles of scientific parsimony and convenience might well lead us to favour the Copernican model as being more useful.

All the foregoing might well be described as a pre-emptive attempt at sociological 'yardarm clearing' or even mystification by sociological astrology and I would now like to hurriedly sketch in a few of the elements that might be suitably included in a total institution model of a ship. Most of these aspects of the model construct derive from Goffman's[3] view of certain organisations as total institutions.

While sociological models are theoretical constructs, many individual aspects or components will of course be abstracted from an appreciation of the subjective social reality of the seaman on ships. That is to say, the local totemism of the natives, their interpretations of shipboard life will make a vital contribution to the model, but to say this is not to be constrained to the local perspective of seamen's interpretations. As should be clear from what I have said previously, I think some attempt at transcendence is necessary for a sociological analysis. Our language game should appreciate, but go beyond the taken for granted 'reality' of, the actors.

The total institution perspective focuses on sociological intra-organisational factors in its explanatory and analytical schema. The major determinants or precipitators of action are seen to lie within the social structure of the organisation. The formal shipboard organisation will define and supply all the immediate needs of people on board. That is to say, definitions of 'reality' and needs tend to be given coherent institutional rather than idiosyncratic personal expression. The institution claims a monopoly of the life space of the individual and isolates him to a high degree from intercourse with the outside world in that there is both geographical and social isolation from other universes of meaning and action.

The basis of the whole organisation of the ship model is the formal allocation of work tasks. There is a highly formalised and institution-alised division of labour, the work is broken down into specific pieces and the work roles are re-integrated into a traditional, rigid and highly predictable whole. Each man has his station and his duty. With this predictability we have a tight formal control structure. All activity is scheduled and regulated and this control constrains all seafarers on board, also the co-ordinating plan implies a significant lack of choice at an individual level. The formal para-military authority or power of the officers, which is backed by powerful legal sanctions, is also based on this work division. Also what we might loosely call the informal power structures are closely linked to the specific division of labour. The routine watch and work system governs not only times of work but also meals, relaxation, leisure and possible social contacts. It is a 24-hour-a-day society and all aspects of life are lived out within the narrow physical confines of the ship. All activity is undertaken in the ever present company of others and personal adjustments and actions in the spheres of work and non-work are likely to be compatible as the systems of social control, power sanctions and values operate in both situations. Formal and informal systems of social control are highly developed and for the duration of the voyage at least there will be little chance to escape constraining pressures and sanctions.

Some systems of collective protective strategy or individual modes of adaptation will grow up to limit or curb the effects of power or formal authority on the group or individual within the shipboard model. Personal solutions such as retreatism may be compared with the development of powerful sub-cultures, especially among ratings. Social distance, especially across the officer/rating divide will also be used as a protective device by groups on each side of that large caste-like social division. Not only is there a powerful normative barrier to social intercourse here on the ship but the forms of social distance are also given physical institutional expression in the provision of separate eating places, cabins and recreational facilities for different ranks which further reduces the possibilities of interaction. This architectural allocation of privilege is so traditional as to be unremarkable to seamen.

As with other rigidly hierarchical systems, such as hospitals for instance, there will be a tight control of communication of both a technical and normative kind. Associated with normative communication control will be a powerful ideology or defining system, directed mainly by those in positions of power.

Comprehensive definitions relating to people, actions, attitudes, motives, seamen, other related occupational groups and what is seen as social 'reality' will be offered. These values and normative expectations have a fairly high degree of coherence and as they are powerfully sanctioned are likely to have considerable impact on young seamen joining the shipboard organisation for the first time. Such expectations and directives will be expressed in face-to-face situations where undetected deviance is difficult.

After that quick look at some possible components that could be articulated into what Goffman would call an instrumental total institution model, I would now like to turn to some specific deprivations that are suggested by such a perspective.

Many of these deprivations may be seen to be directly related to the rigid, powerfully constraining and pervasive nature of the social structure and in particular to the division of labour and associated formal hierarchy. The seaman (using this term to connote all men who work on board the ship—including the Master and cadets) is virtually dependent on institutional arrangements for what limited interaction he has on board. As mentioned, the spheres of work and leisure are fused and populated by the same people and informed by the same attitudes, values and expectations. The ship supplies all the more obvious needs of the seaman and the complementary subjective reality for the seamen is likely to be that the institution should supply those needs.

A total institution perspective makes a taxonomic link between such commonly diverse organisations as ships, mental hospitals, closed religious orders and prisons and in what follows I shall draw mainly on criminological material to illustrate many of the deprivations I see arising from the model.

Gresham Sykes[4] has specified many of the 'pains of imprisonment' suffered by prison inmates and these have been further detailed by Terence and Pauline Morris[5] in their study of Pentonville. The deprivations they describe stem from the character of the prison seen as a total institution and in so far as a merchant ship can be viewed as a total institution some will have relevance for the seaman. These deprivations should be understood as relative deprivations, that is relative to shore occupations.

One of the major differences between prisons and ships is that a seaman freely chooses to sign on a ship, shanghaiing being, one hopes, a practice of the past, and his work and social role on the ship are given a meaningful and 'real' interpretation. That is to say, both he and other people will invest his position and role with validity and he may use it as a basis on which to work out an occupational identity. The prisoner, on the other hand, especially the male prisoner, is deprived of meaningful work on entering prison. This loss of work that is defined as useful may be a threat to the self and help to erode his sense of identity. Even if his previous job was not one that had much potential for providing a positive occupational image it may still have been one of the major means by which he fulfilled his self image as the male provider of his family. However, the occupation of seafaring is one that would seem to be capable of providing a strong work-derived profile or identity. This potential is likely to vary from department to department and possibly between various types of ship, but in general terms the seaman knows who he is and what he is doing and does not suffer alienation in the sense of immediate and short-run meaninglessness. At this point, however, we might speculate upon recent trends in manning and such factors as the speed of turnaround, for instance, might have on the possibility of developing a distinctive identification as a seaman which is subjectively meaningful.

Within the ship men will experience a deprivation of goods and services relative to people in the larger society. Their minimal needs will be catered for but after this there will be a dearth of choice on board. Most of the goods and services of society are not available in the ship; the seaman must take what is provided for him at sea. This deprivation of material goods may be held to be an attack on a person's self concept in a materialistic society such as ours. Individuals rely in varying degrees on their material possessions not only to indicate their position in society but also to provide them with elements of their identity. Personality is not a purely psychological variable but has sociological components and determinants in that any personality structure needs to be viewed in relation to its social matrix and physical environment. Seamen are restricted in individual choice and the possession of many goods which might augment personality and other means of clarifying self identities are likely to be sought.

A further deprivation which occurs within a total institution structure is the deprivation of heterosexual relations. On ships this is not as serious or protracted a loss as in prison as there may be access to the opposite sex in port on a physical basis at least. However this deprivation refers not only to coitus but also to the lack of meaningful male/female social interaction in an all-male social organisation. Sykes has claimed that women as significant others provide much of what Cooley has called the 'looking glass self'. To be cut off from the company of women and be deprived of heterosexual relations may give rise to anxiety about a person's masculinity. Possibly associated with this may be guilt feeling concerning masturbation or homosexual contacts with other men, and even in what is popularly called the 'permissive society' these may give rise to doubt concerning sexual identity. However, visits to ports can provide the seaman with the opportunity to seek at least spasmodic relief from such feelings. A periodic need to overcome such doubts and guilts could possibly be seen as the basis of a psychological interpretation of seamen's traditionally debauched forays ashore.

A seaman's deprivation of liberty is not as absolute as that suffered in some institutional settings, but being on a ship does effectively cut off many social contacts and the possibility of taking part in many shore activities. It also lessens the opportunity of establishing and maintaining meaningful social relationships, but possibly one of the greatest losses is the inability to control outside events. Domestic and family situations cannot be immediately influenced due to lack of information and communication facilities. Within the family, for instance, both everyday running and most important decisions must be taken by individuals other than the seaman.

A further loss in prison is seen to be a deprivation of autonomy, and although ships are not pervaded by bureaucratic rules and restrictions to the same extent there is a gross limitation of choice and action by both work schedules and the work hierarchy. The seaman is continually surrounded by other seamen and even off watch there are no places of secure privacy where other seamen cannot seek him out. There are few ways of escape, even by sickness, from the demands of work and shipmates.

One of the principal deprivations in prisons is the loss of security which is felt by most prisoners who have to live in close proximity with other criminals. There is no escape from possibly exploitive situations, both aggressors and victims will need to live together. On a ship the degree of coercive violence is likely to be small compared with that exercised within a prison community, and while there are not likely to be many who feel physically insecure, a degree of psychological insecurity may well be felt during the young seaman's early life at sea. There will be little exploitation but a great deal of teasing and testing may have to be endured. Failure and success labels tend to stick for the duration of the voyage at least and aggressors and victims will have to live and work together here also.

To the above deprivations which have been described by writers mainly in relation to prison populations, we may add the relative deprivation of various kinds of stimuli. This lack of stimuli is likely to be common to all total institutions and may be looked at under two general headings, a relative deprivation of social stimuli and a relative deprivation of sensory stimuli.

Some items which may be considered under the former heading have been dealt with above. The social structure of the ship does not have the potential richness of relations of the larger social milieux available to the shore worker; as we have said, the element of choice is limited mainly by size, work and norms governing social interaction with the ship. Also lacking are the stimuli provided by family relations, children, wives and friends. However, here the degree of deprivation may depend to some extent on the formal and informal roles played within the institution. Some shipping companies allow masters' and officers' wives to accompany them to sea, but this provision does not usually extend to ratings. In any case the presence of a wife at sea does not constitute a family dyad in the accepted sense. The modes of behaviour and opportunity open to her will depend to a great extent on the rank of her husband. She too will be constrained by the division of labour and work hierarchy. Social stimuli in the form of local and national newspapers, television and radio will also be greatly restricted on the ship.

In most total institutions there is a gross lack of sensory stimuli, but on a ship there is the opportunity to see new places and hear new sounds. This is part of the traditional attraction of seafaring in the first place, but it must be remembered that the seaman sees infinitely more seascapes than strange landscapes, and in many ports shore leave is very restricted. For instance a large tanker on a voyage from the United Kingdom to the Persian Gulf and back round the Cape of Good Hope may be at sea continuously for two and a half months with no chance of shore leave if loading takes place from an offshore submarine pipeline.

However, the main sensory deprivation that a seaman is likely to experience is the lack of physical contact with other individuals. This deprivation is only partly sexual, as mentioned above; on a ship the seaman is not only deprived of the social and physical contact of women that would be available to him in a family situation but also contact with children.

It has been claimed by Spitz[6] that infants deprived of handling over a long period of time are likely to show a great deal of lethargy and possibly sink into an emotional decline. Also part of what is usually called maternal deprivation may well be associated with a lack of sensory stimulation. It is possible that adults subject to sensory deprivations such as a lack of physical contact may suffer depression or even some form of transient psychosis or temporary mental disturbance. The case of a person condemned to solitary confinement might provide the paradigm case of extreme social and sensory deprivation.

The deprivation of physical and social contact with children in a family setting that a seaman experiences has a further dimension in that such situations provide adults with the opportunity of legitimate role releases which may be tension reducing. Playing with young children provides a recognised opportunity for actions which would be viewed as unbecoming or silly and a serious reflection on one's suitability for various roles if they were not performed to amuse children.

It should be borne in mind that not all the deprivations we have looked at will weigh equally heavily on all people subject to them. The extent of deprivation subjectively felt will obviously vary from person to person. Some of the deprivations described above may even be welcome, for instance a deprivation of sexual contacts with women might be seen as a positive relief if there has been previous emotional difficulty associated with heterosexual contacts. Most of the deprivations I have tried to sketch are likely to make some impact on all men on board, but deprivations felt will, among other things, be some function of the formal position occupied within the structure. I have not touched on the deprivations that may be experienced by the formal rigours of the legal disciplinary system, into which a high degree of arbitrary power may enter. That is to say that within the power structure of the total institution we would expect to find a differential incidence and impact of relative deprivation.

The supporting and constraining structure of the total institution which supplies the seaman's needs and limits his decisions and choices is likely to encourage dependence and in this sense it limits his social awareness and maturation. The social structure of the ship is rigidly fixed and clearly delineated, the position and expectations of other people are known or generally predictable, the social reality of the ship is seen in terms of relatively few fixed categories, in which consideration of formal rank and status are prominent.

In the less rigid but more complex social milieux ashore the seaman may well appear to others as immature and he himself may experience a sense of unease and difficulty in communication, he may feel out of place and 'not understood'. The Gallup Poll study of seafarers' attitudes commissioned by the Rochdale Committee[7] found that in their sample a great many seamen find difficulty in 'getting on' with people ashore; 24 per cent of officers and men not on tankers experienced such difficulty and although the men questioned claimed that this was due to the fact that 'people did not understand their lives', it seems as likely from the perspective adopted here to be due to poorly developed social skills caused by the restrictions of the total institution. In this sense the higher figure for tankers, where the effects of the closed community are likely to be more pronounced, is significant, as is the finding that of all categories of seamen deck officers claim to have the greatest difficulty in 'getting on' with people, 34 per cent of the sample in the deck officers department found such difficulty. Deck officers are likely to have been socialised into the shipboard life more rigorously and systematically and at an earlier age than other seamen and so might be seen to experience the deprivations of a total institution to a greater degree than other seamen. Most join ships direct from school or nautical college and only 19 per cent, according to Gallup, had experience of previous jobs, as opposed to 75 per cent of engineer officers.[7]

As Aubert and Arner point out,[8] on the ship the seaman is a mature and responsible man doing a demanding job which is occasionally both difficult and dangerous. However, ashore, he may be seen as immature, perfunctory or show a high degree of social unskilfulness. Literary stereotypes of seamen have often reflected this view. The behaviour of the rough-hewn, jolly, bluff and hearty, but rather simple seaman of popular literature may well be interpreted as a lack of any extensive repertoire of alternative responses, social actions and categorisations which are adequate for the more complex patterns of social relations and interactions ashore where there are less evident authority and positional pegs by which to orient attitudes and behaviour. What we might call social navigation is less easy ashore than in the more stable and predictably stratified environment of the ship.

This immaturity to be sociologically meaningful needs to be related to a specific social situation; on the ship the seaman is 'at home' and sure of his position, work, skills, duties and responsibilities; it is only ashore that a sense of difference and separateness becomes noticeable, and while such a feeling is likely to aid and further a man's identification as a seaman, it also may give rise to feelings of deprivation. His being ill at ease in the shifting, complex and more fluid social world ashore where he may have few significant relationships could, from our model, be due to early and prolonged experience in the total institution setting having led to a relative deprivation of alternative roles, opportunities and interactions.

REFERENCES

1. A. W. Gouldner, 'Metaphysical Pathos and the Theory of Bureaucracy', *American Political Science Review*, Vol. 49, 1955.
2. R. B. Braithewaite, *Scientific Explanation*, 1960. Harper and Row, London.
3. E. Goffman, *Asylums*, Penguin Books, 1968. Harmondsworth.

4. G. M. Sykes, *The Society of Captives*, Princeton University Press, 1964.
5. T. P. and P. Morris, *Pentonville*, London, Routledge & Kegan Paul, 1963; also cf. D. Clemmer, *The Prison Community*, Holt, Rinehart and Winston, New York. D. R. Cressey (ed.), *The Prison*, Holt, Rinehart and Winston, New York, 1961. M. E. Wolfgang, L. Savitz, N. Johnston (eds.), *The Sociology of Punishment and Correction*, John Wiley, New York, 1962.
6. R. A. Spitz, 'Hospitalism', 1945; *The Psychoanalytic Study of the Child*, Vol. 1, No. 1, 1945; also cf. more recent work such as P. Solomon *et al.* (eds.), *Sensory Deprivation*, Harvard University Press, Cambridge, Ma., 1961.
7. *Committee of Inquiry into Shipping* (Rochdale), Cmnd. 4337, London, HMSO, 1970.
8. V. Aubert and O. Arner, 'Work and its Structural Setting', in T. Burns (ed.), *Industrial Man*, Penguin Books, Harmondsworth 1969.

Seven · Some Problems Associated with the Selection and Training of Deck and Engineer Cadets in the British Merchant Navy

WARREN H. HOPWOOD

Traditional manning patterns predominant aboard British Merchant ships call for a division of labour into four main sections, or departments. These are known as the Deck, Engine room, Catering and Radio departments, broadly concerned with navigation and cargo operations, propulsion, domestic services and communications, respectively. Within each department, personnel are formally organised in a rigid hierarchical structure. At the apex of each structure are the ship's officers headed by the Chief Engineer in the Engine room department, the Purser or Chief Steward in the Catering department and the First Radio Officer in the Radio department. The Master of the ship, who has attained his rank as the culmination of his career structure in the Deck department, has certain statutory powers and obligations which include responsibility for the safety of ship, cargo and crew.

All Deck Officers, and a proportion of Engineer Officers begin their careers as Deck Cadets and Engineer Cadets respectively. These Cadets are selected and employed by individual shipping companies and have certain contractual obligations to their employers. In turn, the employer is contractually bound to his Cadets and, among other things, undertakes responsibility for their training. In recent years the shipping industry has suffered increasing recruitment difficulties and a mounting loss of serving personnel; in particular, wastage rates are high and training costs are heaviest[1] in the areas of Deck and Engineer Officer training.

This paper examines the career structures of these grades of personnel, their patterns of initial training and certain problems associated with their adaptation to the shipboard environment. Findings are based upon survey data obtained in 1971 in the substantive area of a large British Nautical school instrumental in the preparation of Cadets for a sea career.

Paradoxically, nothing emerging from the survey data purports to indicate 'cures' for wastage from the sea, for work already carried out in this field suggests that acceptability of a relatively high rate of manpower turnover may be an inevitable feature of future planning by the shipping industry. What does seem to be clear, however, is that a number of factors may be responsible for premature disturbance of an individual's career pattern, however short his term of service may be, and that many of these are capable of exerting powerful influences on his attitude to the sea as a career. Should his own experience at sea be such that he is unable to transmit favourable accounts to new recruits with whom he may sail, or to prospective recruits should he eventually find alternative employment ashore, then future recruitment, both in the short and long term, may be adversely affected. What does emerge from analysis of survey data, however, are a number of causes of individual discontent, and tentative suggestions for their removal are put forward.

TRAINING PATTERNS PAST AND PRESENT

In order to appreciate the connection between certain of the survey findings and the difficulties already mentioned, it is necessary to compare past and present training patterns of Officer Cadets.

Traditionally, the Deck Cadet entered a shore-based residential training establishment direct from his secondary education and spent one year in full-time preparation for a sea career. The course followed was orientated towards specificity of knowledge and skill, and socialisation patterns within such schools purported to be instrumental in the assimilation of the recruit into the occupational group.

Many of these establishments demonstrated explicit homogenising aims; that is to say, the relevance of a Cadet's prior experience was intentionally minimised during the course of his adjustment. The status of a new Cadet was low, but progressively increased as scheduled status passages were successfully accomplished. Cadets wore uniform and were encouraged to develop those qualities held to be desirable in a future Officer, in other words a further homogenising effect was produced where:

> All men must wear identical clothing, have their hair cut in the same way and show similar posture and bearing.[2]

Socialisation processes within such establishments included an element of doctrinal conversion, a social psychological process whereby recruits to an occupation, or profession, come to exchange their own lay views and imagery of the occupation for those the occupation ascribes to itself.[3] The effectiveness of such processes was said to depend upon the entry of a Cadet direct from his secondary education, before his supposed 'contamination' by the attitudes of those already at sea.

Many such training establishments were monotechnic in character and internal organisation was not dissimilar to that found aboard ship; indeed, old vessels moored offshore were occasionally used for the purpose. The Cadets lived on board, 'shore leave' was often infrequent and this, and other deprivations, had the result of attenuating interaction between Cadets and the wider society for an appreciable period of time.

Recently, questions have been asked[4] concerning the relevance of aspects of traditional socialisation processes to present-day requirements at sea; a more recent view[5] expresses the opinion that considerable educational and social advantages would result from the integration of nautical schools with establishments catering for a wider range of disciplines. These and other external social pressures have resulted in a movement of the schools along a homogenising-differentiating continuum in the direction of greater differentiation; that is to say, greater account is now being taken of the interests and different background of each Cadet, while explicit procedures purporting to accelerate the doctrinal conversion of Cadets are far less obvious than was the case in traditional training methods.

By contrast, present-day patterns of Deck Officer training, recently introduced, take a markedly different form. A recruit now seeks employment as a Cadet at the termination of his secondary education and then follows a two-week Induction Course. During this course he is made aware of aspects of organisational structure of the Merchant Navy, shipboard safety, personnel management and elementary seamanship. He then goes to sea for several voyages (Initial Sea Period) in a period of about one year and returns to a training establishment to spend six months following a shore-based training scheme (Phase I). After the successful completion of this phase, the Cadet makes several more voyages in a period of about one year (Phase II) at the end of which time he returns to his training establishment for a further six months to complete shore-based training (Phase III). At the end of Phase III, he sits either the Ordinary National Certificate (ONC) or Ordinary National Diploma (OND) examinations leading to exemptions from statutory examinations for Deck Officers.

For the Engineer Officer recruit the traditional method of entry, and often his first introduction to the sea, was as a Junior Engineer after having completed a craft apprenticeship of at least four years' duration in a marine or other engineering workshop. It has been estimated that some 80 per cent of engineer officers are still recruited in this way.

In 1952 the Alternative Entry Scheme (The Engineer Cadet Training Scheme) was devised as a new approach to the supply of suitable men for the more complex ships entering service. Three normal phases of training constitute this Scheme. The first of these follows immediately upon the Cadet's secondary education and takes place in a shore-based establishment, such as a technical college. Here he undertakes a course of two years' duration leading to one of various examinations such as the OND, or the Marine Engineering Technicians Certificate (METC) of the City & Guilds of London Institute. Success in such examinations affords certain exemptions from statutory examinations for Engineer Officers. The second phase of training consists of a period of about one year at sea as a Cadet Engineer, at the end of which time he returns to a shore-based establishment for a further year to complete his training.

A feature of both past and present training schemes for Deck Cadets is that the Cadet is obliged to reside at the training establishment during all shore-based phases of training. On the other hand this has never been the case for Engineer Cadets. Nevertheless, in 1966 and ensuing years several sections of the shipping industry in consultation with a small number of large training establishments set up residential courses populated by Deck and Engineer Cadets alike. These Joint Training Schemes were held to foster understanding between Cadets following courses in the two disciplines, and to lead to closer co-operation between Deck and Engine Room departments aboard ship. Such co-operation is considered to be a prerequisite for efficient ship operation.

A feature of the original Joint Training Schemes, although the differential phasing of Deck and Engineer Cadet training patterns led to certain difficulties, was that Cadets entered their courses direct from secondary school. It was, therefore, possible to subject all Cadets to common socialisation processes held to be appropriate to their future roles. At the training establishment studied, a Joint Training Scheme was in operation and although different syllabus requirements demanded different specialisation patterns for each group, sufficient common ground was found to exist to allow the formation of a small number of heterogeneous teaching groups; additionally, further formal and informal arrangements resulted in opportunities for interaction between Deck and Engineer Cadets for a large proportion of the course time.

With the inception of new patterns of Deck Cadet training, serious difficulties arose for establishments in which such Joint Training Schemes were conducted. Common socialisation processes could no longer be applied to both Deck and Engineer Cadets as the former had now experienced life at sea prior to entering, whereas the latter continued to enter from secondary education. At the time of writing, some confusion exists in the minds of those concerned with training of this kind, for it seems clear that Joint Training Schemes can no longer be conducted in their original form. It would also seem that the new movement of the Deck Cadet towards a form of 'on-the-job training' as a first introduction to sea life is in conflict with any general aim of the Merchant Navy Deck Officer group towards a greater level of professionalisation. Paradoxically, initial training of similar form, a feature of traditional Engineer Officer recruit entry, was significantly omitted from the newer Alternative Entry Scheme.

THE INSTITUTIONAL NATURE OF THE SHIP

In seeking a model of institutional life against which to view the shipboard environment, a review of literature reveals that little is known of the sociological perspective of the ship, or of patterns of interaction of the various groups forming her crew.

Anecdotally, some ships are said to be 'happy', while others are not, but factors contributing to either situation are not easy of explanation. What is clear, however, is that a ship's crew constitutes a largely random selection of individuals, the majority of whom are unknown to each other until the moment of commencing a voyage. When the ship leaves port, these individuals are encapsulated by their shipboard environment, often for long periods of time; the internal social system of the ship is cut off from the wider society both by distance and by physical barriers. At sea, all aspects of life for the seamen are conducted in the same place with close scheduling of all phases of activity and, to a lesser extent, the same may be said of periods spent in port. The seaman lives at his place of work and, in addition to his work periods, is forced to take his leisure with fellow-workers and with his superiors. When at sea opportunities for heterosexual interaction are limited, and sexual deprivation is a familiar occupational characteristic. Periods of absence from home raise difficulties for the individual who wishes to pursue a meaningful family life. Thus, although crew members may be drawn from many different levels of society, and occupy different hierarchical positions on board, they are so to speak 'all in the same boat' in the sense that, from the shipmaster to the most lowly member of crew, few are immune from those characteristics apparently inherent as shipboard life.

Those same characteristics may be contrasted with basic social arrangements in modern society whereby the individual tends to change his environment for different phases of activity such as sleep, work and leisure. Furthermore, such activities need not necessarily follow a rational plan, may be conducted under a different authority and may be shared with different co-participants.

Many features of life aboard ship are to be found in a small number of other institutional settings. These include logging camps, military bases, prisons, mental hospitals, monasteries, convents and some boarding schools seen as members of a category referred to as 'total' institutions.[7]

Such institutions serve markedly different purposes ranging from care and protection, to the restriction of movement of individuals thought to be a threat or a danger to society. An institutional aim may be the further socialisation of those passing through, or of resocialisation where the formal aim is to make up for, or to correct, some deficiency in earlier socialisation. On the other hand, institutions such as logging camps, military bases and ships have, traditionally, justified their existence only on the instrumental grounds of efficient technical task performance.

A feature common to such institutions is an explicit training purpose but, for all members of her crew, this cannot be said of the ship. Again, the general aims of many institutions purport to change, model and reshape individuals and thus affect the total person. It has been considered, however, that profound contradictions and tensions in a seaman's role derive from his membership of an institution which takes no conscious responsibility for the function of influencing personality and identity, a deficiency recognised by Brassey[8] nearly a century ago:

> The shipowner and Captain, who do nothing for the mental welfare of their seamen, have forgotten the most important part of their outfit.

The extent to which comparisons can be drawn between an individual institution and Goffman's model, that is to say the 'totality' of an institution, depends upon its permeability.

Permeability is an indicator of the influence exerted upon the institutional society by that existing 'outside'; the higher the level of permeability, the greater the similarity between the institutional and external society and the fewer the tensions experienced by its members.

It might be expected that low levels of permeability are characteristic of oil tankers both at sea and in port, where time is cut to a minimum by high-speed cargo handling techniques and tanker terminals, often situated in positions governed by safety requirements and deep-sea access, afford little opportunity for social interaction between local populations and tanker crews. On the other hand, passenger liners possibly enjoy a high level of permeability in that their social systems are, in many respects, microcosms of wider society. However, for reasons now to be considered, there may well be individuals who seek out environments of low permeability and obtain maximum satisfaction from living and working therein.

PROBLEMS OF ADAPTATION

The relative isolation of ships' crews from the wider society is significant when considering their modes of adaptation to shipboard environment. For many, and for various reasons, few problems may exist. For example, there are good reasons to suppose that the isolated nature of the ship is attractive to many who find difficulty in adjusting to life in the wider society; amongst these will be individuals with pronounced deviant tendencies, and others perhaps from impoverished social backgrounds who regard life aboard ship an an improvement upon their previous situations. This latter possibility was illuminated during the recent study[9] in which officer recruits from Ireland and Africa regarded life at sea as superior, in terms of opportunity for social interaction and career prospects, to the relatively deprived way of life which they assumed lay ahead of them in their home countries. Similarly,

Shetland youths recruited into the British Merchant Service are apparently not much threatened by the cramped, arduous life on board because island life is even more stunted. They make uncomplaining sailors because, from their point of view, they have little to complain about.[10]

Paradoxically, despite all attempts to devise initial selection procedures, there is a strong possibility that involuntary secondary selection will occur. In other words those remaining at sea after the age of about thirty years may well include a high proportion of crew members who, for reasons already stated, may have few adaptation problems.

Concerning modes of adaptation, that is to say the various ways in which a recruit comes to terms with life aboard ship and succeeds in reducing tensions between his life 'inside', and society 'outside', an ideal goal may be the construction by the recruit of a reasonably stable existence from the resources of the ship itself; this possibility is enhanced by any improvement in the quality of life on board.

However, there appears to be little justification for the assumption that a mode of adaptation, once achieved, remains constant over time. A stable mode of adaptation may be transformed into one of intransigence, or of 'tankeritis',[11] a form of situation withdrawal known by different names in different institutions. In these circumstances, a man may relinquish his sea career at any point, often for reasons seemingly disproportionate to the financial and other sacrifices involved. Such shift of emphasis from one mode of adaptation to another, apparently from a relatively stable mode to one of intransigence in this case, is illuminated by the following comment:

> On the first ship I was on, the Chief Officer left the sea. He had been on board for some months and his wife had a child while he was away and the Company couldn't send out a relief for him. He was very upset about it and this may have changed his mind about the sea.[12]

For the small number of Cadets aboard a ship, a special problem may exist. While not yet qualified Officers, they are aligned more with the Officers of the ship than with the ratings, with whom they are often discouraged from forming particularistic bonds. In this sense, they occupy a marginal position and are often forced to turn towards each other for companionship and common interests. As one Cadet remarked:

> I found it difficult to strike a balance between Officers and ratings; this is where the training let me down. I didn't know

how to treat a rating. A Cadet is in an awkward position between Officers and ratings.[13]

ATTITUDES OF CADETS TO CAREER CHOICE

In spite of a number of difficulties already mentioned, it should not be inferred that ships of the British Merchant Navy are populated by large numbers of unhappy or disillusioned Cadets, at least not during the early stages of their seafaring careers. Survey data revealed, however, a significantly different approach to career choice on the part of Deck Cadets and Engineer Cadets, together with a marked attitude change in the case of the former as the career pattern developed. Cadets in the survey sample were found to have origins in all levels of the status hierarchy with by far the greater proportion originating from the lower-middle and skilled working classes in approximately equal proportions. Some 50 per cent of the sample came from family backgrounds with seafaring connections; in the case of Deck Cadets, these connections were with shipmasters or Deck Officers, and where the family seafaring connections showed a strong bias towards engineering, the Cadet chose an engineering course.

(a) *Deck Cadets*

For a majority of Deck Cadets in the sample, the choice of sea career had stemmed from one or another earlier frustrations such as unwillingness to embark upon sixth-form studies, failure to complete 'A'-Level courses, failure to gain entry to the career of first choice or problems created by the breakdown of family life. Many regarded participation in officer training as an honourable exit from the scene of an apparent failure. On the other hand, there were those Cadets, mainly those who had lived in close proximity to the sea for an appreciable period of time, who had made the sea their first career. choice. Also, as mentioned earlier, the career choice of African and Irish Cadets in the sample was looked upon as an 'escape-route' from the relative social deprivation and poor career prospects in their country of origin.

Notwithstanding these findings, however, Deck Cadets returning to shore-based training after their first few months at sea generally expressed satisfaction with their choice of career. After a further period of sea-service significant changes in attitude were revealed by data obtained during the second period of shore-based training.

In many cases Cadets regretted abandoning 'A'-Level courses and generally demonstrated a high incidence of disappointment and disillusionment with their choice of career. African and Irish Cadets continued to be satisfied, for reasons already stated, as did Cadets able to satisfy minimum entry requirements with C.S.E. qualifications, or G.C.E. 'O'-Level passes of relatively low grade.

(b) *Engineer Cadets*

In contrast to recruits to Deck courses, who gave few positive reasons for career choice, the choice of engineering was predominant and deliberate in the case of Engineer Cadets, many of whom stated that the development of engineering interests began for them at an early age.

However, the survey revealed what might be termed the 'Alternative Entry Paradox'; that is to say, in nearly every case the choice of a sea career was stated to rest upon the opportunity for world travel, associated with the opportunity to participate in a more prestigious form of engineering training than could be obtained elsehwere. Exceptions were found among Cadets following the lower-level M.E.T.C. course who appeared to be as interested in becoming ship's Officers as they were in engineering. These Cadets admitted to being pleased with the career opportunities held out to them in view of their relatively modest entry qualifications.

(c) *Career Development*

In general, and despite growing disillusionment, Deck Cadets saw themselves remaining at sea at least until they obtained Master's Certificates at the age of about twenty-five. Few Engineer Cadets were able to look that far ahead, refusing to commit themselves until they had sampled sea life. There was little undue concern with the possibility that adaptation problems might arise for, should these be insurmountable, work on land would be easy to find with the qualifications gained from attendance at the shore-based establishment. At the same time, these respondents were critical of a training pattern that did not admit the possibility of sampling sea life until their period of initial training was virtually completed.

ATTITUDES OF CADETS TO ACADEMIC WORK
AND INITIAL SOCIALISATION

One purpose of the survey referred to in this paper was an investigation of attitudes to academic work, and to initial socialisation processes, as experienced by Deck and Engineer Cadets in a large British shore-based training establishment. Although samples of Deck Cadets reflected all stages of their training, this was not the case for Engineer Cadets, for the establishment concerned offered only the initial two years of shore-based training. It was, therefore, not possible to sample Engineer Cadets with sea experience for, as has already been stated, the Engineer Cadet participating in the Alternative Entry Scheme does not go to sea until his two-year course has been completed. Nevertheless, as this part of the survey was concerned with attitudes to ongoing initial training, sample deficiency of this kind was considered to be acceptable, provided that Engineer Cadets were not called upon to assess the relevance of their training to life at sea. In the event, however, this difficulty diminished in importance as data accumulated. What transpired to be their prime concern was the relevance of academic work to engineering in general, and to obtaining engineering qualifications in particular; in these matters they were prepared to rely upon the knowledge and experience of their teachers. Engineer Cadets were generally highly motivated towards the academic content of their courses in contrast to their low motivation towards becoming ship's Officers. A partial explanation of this may lie in the training patterns themselves which provide courses eventually leading to membership of a professional body and a future career which may lie in one of many different areas of the engineering field.

Although the Engineering OND and the Deck OND demand roughly equivalent attendance in terms of teaching hours, an Engineer Cadet spends 84 weeks in a shore-based school, whereas a Deck Cadet spends only 44 or 52 weeks in the same establishment. Furthermore, the attendance of the former is broken only by normal school holidays, whereas the attendance of the latter is interrupted by two periods at sea each of about one year in duration. On these grounds, Engineer Cadets in the survey sample were critical of Deck courses, and pointed to the educational advantages inherent in their own courses which provided greater continuity of shore-based training. The Deck courses were not seen to have any real worth apart from a direct application to a sea career.

Paradoxically, Deck Cadets took an opposite view and seriously questioned the relevance of their own academic courses to a sea career. Data provided strong indications that the OND and ONC schemes were thought by these Cadets to be divorced from a realistic appreciation of the role of the Deck Officer. On this point it is impossible to comment other than to observe that Deck courses, and their appropriate entry requirements, seem to have been established by a multiplicity of individuals and organisations not necessarily closely involved with Cadet training and whose members may not have served at sea for many years, if at all. Furthermore, as no basis for course design seems to be available in terms of job specification or other research data, it is almost inevitable that questions of relevance should arise in the minds of these recruits.

As far as initial socialisation processes are concerned, from the perspective of the participants these were largely seen to constitute 'good training', but were otherwise held to be irrelevant to sea life. By this was meant that life in the school's residential units prepared Cadets for communal living afloat, and that encouragement towards relatively high standards of personal hygiene and order was in the common interest.

By contrast, the demands of the school relating to the wearing of uniform, standards of civilian dress, regulation of leisure time and general regulations governing conduct held to be appropriate to future Officers, were generally seen as irrelevant to life at sea, by those Cadets with sea experience. On the other hand, a number of Cadets without sea experience stated that they had been attracted to a sea career by expectations of the demands of what they had considered to be a para-military organisation. Nevertheless, almost without exception, Cadets considered themselves to be members of a special organisation, and tended to resist integration with students of other departments of the large college of which the school was a part. In the words of one respondent, typical of many:

> We are totally different from these people. I don't see myself as being the same type of student as they are.[14]

SOME CONSEQUENCE FOR RECRUITMENT

As stated at the outset, analysis of the survey data does not illuminate ways and means by which manpower wastage from the Merchant Navy may, in the short term, be arrested and reversed. However, there are strong indications that a number of factors are responsible for a high degree of disillusionment and disappointment among Cadets and, by inference, among qualified Officer personnel.

Many studies of so-called wastage problems tend to under-emphasise the effects upon new Cadets of unfavourable impressions of a sea career from those with whom they first sail. Furthermore, it is of some importance to a prospective Cadet that he does not receive unfavourable impressions of sea life from seafarers, or from ex-seafarers, prior to committing himself to a sea career. Links between prospective Cadets and serving or ex-seafarers were clearly visible in survey data; in the case of Engineer Cadets, opinions obtained were generally favourable towards an engineering career. For Deck Cadets, advice given by serving Deck Officers, or by ex-Deck Officers, was generally discouraging, although other factors associated with career choice, as mentioned earlier, were apparently strong enough to overcome such discouragement. Nevertheless, at a later stage of career development, some Deck Cadets regretted that they had not taken earlier advice and sought alternative careers. What the survey could not reveal, however, was the number of pro-spective Cadets who, by virtue of such discouragement, did not come forward for training.

It is now of interest to consider reasons why a relatively high pro-portion of Deck Cadets become dissatisfied with their choice of career. Such reasons constituted well-defined and 'saturated'[15] categories of data, but because of the complexity of the problem it cannot be claimed that the reasons given are by any means ex-haustive.

(a) *Relative Deprivation*

Whatever model of shipboard life is constructed, there are certainly elements of relative deprivation experienced by most seafarers. Here it is impossible to generalise, although a common linking thread would seem to be the inability of seafarers to lead meaningful family lives. The current 'solution' lies in the manipulation of permeability levels on board including, at least in the case of Officer personnel, the increasing tendency of Shipping Companies to permit wives to accompany their husbands on voyages; the significance for the partners concerned is reduced, however, when child-rearing, of necessity ashore, becomes the wife's predominant role.

Permeability may be raised in other ways; for example, by provid-ing space and equipment for various forms of recreation. Generally speaking, respondents indicated that such provision was adequate and that good use was made of the facilities available.

(b) *Changes in Personal Circumstances*

The attitude of an individual to his sea career, and his mode of adaptation to shipboard life, may be affected by changes in his personal circumstances. Such changes may be brought about by the ill health of the individual or of members of his family, marriage, birth, bereavement, financial gains or losses, housing problems and so on. Paradoxically, it would also be necessary to consider changes brought about by, in the case of a married Officer, his wife being unable to continue to sail with him.

Factors such as these might form the basis of a 'personal change inventory' for each crew member. Continuous collection of such data, together with suitable follow-up studies, may then lead to the development of a 'change index' from which could be predicted disturbances in tension patterns between a seafarer and his home environment. Action by management when such an index approached critical values might then avert the possibility of the movement of the seafarer towards a less favourable adaptation mode.

It is interesting to note that an effect of changes in traditional training patterns of Deck Cadets is the transference of early adaptation problems from the shore-based establishment to the ship. In this sense, there is now little difference between Deck Cadets and young crew members recruited as ratings who, after a brief induction period, make the transition from school to ship; in some respects, the latter may be better equipped for change of this kind.

Important questions that must be asked concern the extent to which shipboard organisation has been modified to accommodate such changes in training patterns. For example, are there those on board with responsibility for the welfare of young crew members? If so, to what extent are they now additionally equipped to solve adaptation problems which, until recently, have been the province of trained and experienced members of Staff of shore-based establishments?

(c) *Initial Selection*

Present indications from a number of sources suggest that there are certain groups of individuals who remain contented with life at sea for an appreciable period of time. Among these might be included those attracted to the relative isolation of the ship, those who find

difficulty in adjusting to the norms of wider society, perhaps display-
ing homosexual, alcoholic or other deviant tendencies, those with
disturbed home backgrounds and groups whose normal societies
hold promise of greater deprivation than that found aboard ship.
Additionally, in the survey, Deck and Engineer Cadets with the
lowest entry qualifications saw for themselves a long-term future as
ship's Officers.

If survey data relating to career choice has been correctly interpreted, so called 'selection' procedures must be seriously questioned
except, perhaps, the selection of Engineer Cadets for mechanical
aptitude by means of appropriate tests.

For both Deck and Engineer Cadets selection is limited to those
with specific subject combinations at the Ordinary Level of the
General Certificate of Education. These combinations are such that
the shipping industry is in direct competition for recruits with
industry in general, the armed forces and other organisations with
science orientated entry standards. It follows, therefore, that the shipping industry is able to recruit only a small proportion of an already
small percentage of the school-leaving population in a given year.

Even so, it is indeed open to question whether academic screening,
physiological screening or, in the case of Engineer Cadets, screening
procedures for mechanical aptitude, is sufficient to ensure an individual's easy transition from shore to ship and his subsequent
adaptation to sea life. Little is known of the exact nature of childhood limitations on later-life socialisation and it is perhaps for this
reason that occupational role-socialisation is often biased towards
the inculcation of the overt behaviour patterns of the role, rather than
in the direction of attempts to influence fundamental motivation,
or basic values. Alternatively, society may be prepared to consider
conforming behaviour alone as satisfactory evidence of socialisation but, in so doing, must be prepared to accept the risk of the rapid
breakdown of conformity if the individual is placed in a conflict or
stress situation. Such an alternative would generally be unacceptable
for the Merchant Navy Officer, and for individuals in the military
and other special organisations, where incorrect responses to stress
situations could well lead to considerable destruction of life and
property.[16] In this respect a gulf is seen[17] between soldiers, sailors
and airmen, and those in other occupations; as the former must function in situations of terror and panic that naturally make for least
efficient action, something more than intellect[18] is looked for in
Officer recruits.

If this is indeed the case, it is all the more unfortunate that residual Cadet numbers, after physiological and academic screening procedures have taken place, barely match demand. In this event, procedures designed to exclude individuals on the grounds of psychological unsuitability may well result in a reduction of Cadet numbers below the point where a sufficient supply of Officers could be guaranteed for future ship manning. The issue is further complicated in that individual shipping companies, engaged upon a widely differing range of trades with ships of all types, are unwilling to accept a stereotypical Officer whose training pattern might be decided on a national basis.

It seems, therefore, that recruits 'selected' by the methods described must include many who are grossly unsuited in other ways to life at sea and whose subsequent frustration could well lead to a relatively high incidence of occupational psychosis.

With a dilemma of this nature now facing the British shipping industry, there is little room for manoeuvre. A possible solution could lie in the direction of selection from a broader band of academic attainment, together with the design of lower level courses to provide a supply of Officers capable of performing limited executive functions. From this larger number of potential Cadets, it might then be possible to seriously approach the development of selection procedures designed to screen out those whose personal qualities are considered to be unacceptable.

(d) *Academic Courses*

As mentioned earlier, Engineer Cadets in the survey sample did not, in general, question the relevance of their courses. It must be remembered, however, that these respondents were considering relevance to general engineering training and not to an engineering training specifically orientated towards a marine specialisation. Exceptions to this view were again found in data collected from METC course respondents who were of the opinion that their course content was theoretically orientated at the expense of craft skills thought to be a necessary part of a marine engineer's training.

On the other hand, Deck Cadets with sea experience seriously questioned the relevance of their academic courses, finding difficulty in relating the appropriateness of their courses of study to the role of the serving Officer. Many respondents felt themselves inadequately equipped in the areas of seamanship, collision avoidance techniques, navigation and chartwork, subjects assuming diminishing importance in terms of the syllabus content of new courses. To some extent this view was shared by members of the School Staff, and to a greater extent by shipping company training officers whose opinions were canvassed.

In constructing the edifice of new courses for Deck Cadets, it appears that little account was taken of the nature of the Deck Officer's role, a feature which became immediately obvious to many respondents when demands made upon them at sea were seen to bear little or no relationship to the expectations fostered by their academic studies. Frustration born of such circumstances might be expected to create adaptation difficulties for the individual concerned.

The design of lower level courses for certain grades of Deck Officers, aligned firmly with job-analysis and specification, may well remove much of such frustration pointed up by survey data.

(e) *Initial Socialisation*

A view generally held by respondents affirmed the relevance of residential life at the school to life aboard ship. Similarly, socialisation processes designed to develop characteristics such as punctuality, personal cleanliness and the ability to live harmoniously with others were seen to be a necessary part of initial training.

Less acceptable were processes held to foster qualities of leadership, those concerned with the wearing of uniform and processes purporting to develop 'Officer-like' qualities. Many of those were seen as anachronistic, relating more to theoretical requirements of the school, and of the sponsoring shipping companies, than to the realities of life aboard ship.

As with initial selection, there is little agreement between individual shipping companies on a common policy for Officer training and, if respondents from different companies are to be believed, wide variations in expectations of norms of behaviour of Officers from company to company. If this is the case, then an initial training establishment would be expected to find increasing difficulty in the maintenance of socialisation processes applicable to all recruits. Additionally, as mentioned earlier, further difficulties are experienced in schools where approximately one half of the Cadet body has recent experience of life in the industrial setting, the other half, none.

It would seem, therefore, that one of several possibilities must be explored to ensure that Cadets do not become increasingly disillusioned with career choice in the course of their initial training.

Either the industry itself must put forward a common policy for initial socialisation or, should this prove not to be possible, groups of companies may work in close co-operation with selected establishments in pursuit of common aims. Another course of action would seem to lie in the direction of shore-based establishments relinquishing responsibility for all but the academic content of courses, leaving the initial socialisation of Cadets to their respective employers. Should neither possibility be acceptable or practicable, an extreme step may be the replacement of the traditional Cadet entry scheme. Proponents of any new scheme might profitably consider the notion of a novitiate in the form of a probationary period for the new recruit, a characteristic not unknown in recruitment patterns of other closed or semi-closed communities with voluntary entrance.

CONCLUSIONS

The main inferences from data collected in the substantive area of the survey indicate several factors opposing a Cadet's assimilation into his occupational group, his contentment with career choice and the development of favourable impressions of a sea career.

For reasons of sample deficiency already mentioned, further research is necessary in order to explore the attitudes of Engineer Cadets to a sea career after some experience at sea has been gained. It might be speculated, however, that they would still feel themselves to be 'free' men in the sense that they could leave the sea at any time, and find immediate employment ashore. For the Engineer Cadet, assimilation into the occupational group of the seafarer does not seriously arise, whereas assimilation into the occupational group of the engineer is of considerable importance. In contrast, the Deck Cadet has not the Engineer Cadet's awareness of direction. He is uncertain of the nature of his role, for this has not been defined. His new form of training appears to lead him away from ultimate professional status and, unlike the Engineer Cadet, he does not identify himself with any group in wider society.

For the shipping industry it is of some importance that Deck Cadets, and Deck Officers, should not experience unsurmountable adaptation difficulties for, should they feel themselves trapped by their environment, they may make irrational career decisions in order to gain their 'freedom'. Adaptation problems may well show a marked decrease if selection criteria other than an individual's mere academic ability are employed; if care is taken by employers to appreciate circumstances leading to an increase of tension between a seafarer's shipboard and home environment; and if the permeability level of the shipboard environment is raised as far as is practicable.

Of no less importance to the shipping industry is the dissatisfaction of the Deck Cadet with his initial training, both in terms of academic content and socialisation processes. Survey data revealed that many respondents were unable to reconcile much of the academic content of their courses with the observed role of the Deck Officer. In particular, they found difficulty in relating the depth of scientific study required by their courses to a Deck Officer's daily round.

In spite of this, however, there can be little doubt that the growing complexity of ships and shipboard equipment must necessitate the provison of specialist courses for some Deck Officers. At the same time, all Deck Officers must possess a greater degree of practical expertise than has traditionally been demanded in the areas of safety, collision avoidance procedures, navigation, environmental studies and general seamanship; and a junior Officer is called upon to demonstrate this expertise from the moment he steps aboard his first ship. Furthermore, such performance is frequently used by his superiors to assess his usefulness. In the views of many respondents, their common training did not lead towards the satisfaction of observed demands in the industrial setting, but towards the acquisition of other knowledge for which demands were not made. If opinions of this kind are representative of a more general feeling among Deck Cadets, and junior Deck Officers, then a further factor contributing to the onset of disillusionment has been revealed. In these circumstances, it becomes a matter of some urgency to investigate relationships beween a Deck Officer's training and his job-satisfaction, and to question the justification of present arrangements whereby all Officer recruits are given a costly training on the assumption that they are all to become shipmasters.

If follow-up studies of METC Engineer Cadets, and Deck Cadets with low-grade passes at GCE 'O' Level, show that members of these groups continue to be satisfied with career choice, it may transpire that the shipping industry could be well served by a considerable number of Deck Officers recruited at lower levels. These Officers would be highly trained practical men, able to perform a range of limited executive functions.

If, at the same time, selection methods were developed to take greater account of the matching of the prospective Cadet to his future shipboard environment, it is tempting to speculate that a greater degree of compatibility might be expected than was evident from analysis of data from the present survey.

REFERENCES

1. *Report of the Committee of Inquiry into Shipping* (The Rochdale Report), HMSO London, paragraph 870, 1970.
2. O. G. Brim, and S. Wheeler, *Socialization after Childhood*, New York, John Wiley & Sons, 1966.
3. F. Davis, 'Professional Socialization as Subjective Experience', in H. S. Becker *et al.*, *Institutions and the Person*, Aldine Publishing Co., Chicago, 1968.
4. *Parliamentary Debates—Commons* (Hansard), Vol. 773, 11 November–22 November, 1968-9.
5. Rochdale Report, op. cit., paragraph 912.
6. G. Harries-Jenkins, 'Professionals in Organizations', in J. A. Jackson, *Professions and Professionalization*, Cambridge University Press, 1970.
7. E. Goffman, *Asylums*, Doubleday, New York, 1961.
8. T. Brassey, *British Seamen*, Longmans Green & Co., London, 1877, p. 62.
9. W. H. Hopwood, 'Preparing to be a Merchant Navy Officer: A study in occupational socialization' (M. Ed. Dissertation, Bristol University, unpublished, 1971).
10. E. Goffman, op. cit., p. 66.
11. E. Goffman, op. cit.
12. W. H. Hopwood, op. cit., p. 81.
13. Ibid., p. 8.
14. Ibid., p. 36.
15. B. G. Glaser, and A. L. Strauss, *The Discovery of Grounded Theory*, Weidenfeld & Nicolson, London, 1968.
16. R. R. Dynes, *Organized Behaviour in Disaster*, Heath Lexington Books, London, 1970.
17. C. Barnett, *Governing Elites: Studies in training and selection*, Oxford University Press, New York, 1969, p. 196.
18. Ibid., p. 197.

Eight · External Control and Organisational Adaptability: American, British and Spanish Merchant Marine Academies

WILLIAM R. ROSENGREN AND MICHAEL S. BASSIS*

All modern nations train personnel to operate fleets of commercial vessels with which to engage in international trade. Merchant marine personnel are trained for employment aboard ships of three principal types. Although there is enormous variation, in kind and size, within these types, merchant vessels may be characterised as floating resort-hotels designed to accommodate and entertain passengers, as floating warehouses for the temporary storage of goods while in movement over the water, or as gigantic oil tanks in which huge volumes of fluids are moved over the surface of the oceans. The first may range in size from the gigantic Queen Elizabeth II to smaller dry cargo freighters with but a half-dozen cabins for passengers. The latter may range from highly automated modern tankers of the 200,000-ton class which ply the long-distance trades and which take on and discharge petroleum without ever entering port, to smaller ships on the coastal trade which may be in and out of port every few days. In addition, most national fleets contain some extremely modern vessels as well as older ships which may have been in service for twenty-five or more years. But in spite of variations such as these in ship size, state of equipment and machinery, and transport function, the technological knowledge needed to move such ships from port to port is basically identical. Moreover, as Hopwood and others have pointed out, the division of labour aboard ships of all countries reflect these commonalities.[1]

Among the officers who run these vessels are the members of the 'Deck', or 'Navigating', Department who are responsible for the

---

* The authors are much in debt to the many persons associated with nautical education in America, Britain and Spain who gave willingly of their time answering our questions, and allowed their knowledge of the subject to be recorded on tape. We shall follow the custom

general supervision of the accurate movement of the ship from place to place, for the legalities involved in entering and departing foreign ports, for the maintenance of shipboard order, and for the loading, storage and unloading of cargoes. The basic scientific knowledge demanded of these officers are mainly in the fields of mathematics, physics and astronomy which become translated into practical technologies of navigation, shiphandling and cargo and fuel storage, etc. The captain is in overall charge and oversees the work of a few other similarly trained personnel to whom various 'deck' tasks are delegated. These 'officers', in turn, supervise the manual labour undertaken by the 'hands' or 'ratings'. Though marine economics and accounting are more complex than this, the primary responsibility of the Navigating Department is to direct the movement of the ship from place to place in such a fashion so as to realise a profit level acceptable to the operators of the ship. The Engineering Department is charged with the responsibility of caring for the operation, maintenance and repair of the ship's engines and such other mechanical and electrical equipment as might be used to propel the vessel. Again, the theoretical–scientific base for this work must be translated into basic tool-working skills suitable for the task of operating and maintaining the mechanical equipment which drives the ship.

Inasmuch as both the theoretical knowledge and practical skills needed for nautical navigation and engineering are common to all merchant vessels, a matter of considerable sociological interest is the cross-national differences in the organisations maintained in each nation to train personnel to operate such ships. This discussion intends to provide a general description and explanation of differences in the organisation of merchant marine training schools in three countries, the USA, Great Britain and Spain, each of which is involved in preparing personnel for the operation of common navigating and engineering technologies aboard ship. The aim is to offer some illustrative data concerning the social forces at work

---

of maintaining both institutional and personal anonymity. This deprives nautical school administrative officers, faculty members, students, shipping company personnel, and others from seeing their names in print. In compensation for this loss, anonymity may shield them from embarrassment and protect them from assuming responsibility should what is written here turn out to be an inaccurate representation of the situations in which they work.

country resulting in the creation of distinctive modes of nautical training.[2]

The USA, Great Britain and Spain provide a unique basis for comparison in this regard because they dramatise differences in the market environments for which merchant marine officers are produced and to which school activity is primarily addressed. From such a point of view, nautical schools such as these may be conceived as production units, each with unique student-processing problems and with distinctive market situations.

The contrasting markets for ships' officers trained in these three countries offer the most fundamental point of comparison: The number of berths available to newly graduated American marine officers is declining sharply, due not only to the shrinking of the American fleet and the decreasing ratio of personnel required to operate larger modern vessels, but also to the power of maritime labour unions to restrict the numbers of ships' officers permitted to enter the market. This steadily declining market poses critical adaptation and survival problems for the American academies, which must either decrease their output of graduates or locate new markets in which to place them.

Spain represents the opposite type in the sense that its markets for school graduates have increased markedly over the past few years. Not only has the Spanish merchant fleet doubled in the past decade; navigators and engineers from Spanish nautical schools are now being exported for employment aboard ships of foreign flags. The presence of these new markets has created different kinds of organisational problems for, and responses by, the Spanish training academies which must rapidly increase their output of trained personnel.

The market for graduates of British schools is at a point mid-way between these two extremes. Numerous estimates suggest that only a very minor percentage decrease will occur over the next decade in the need for newly trained Merchant Navy officers in Great Britain.[3] But although the market is predicted to continue in a relatively stable state of size for the foreseeable future, it is also a market which is increasingly subjected to economies of costs on the one hand, and rapid technological sophistication on the other. Out of this combination of factors arises a paradox for the British training situation: the pressure is to devise a training formula which will produce at a minimum cost a relatively stable supply of officers with increased technical capabilities and occupationally transferable skills. At first glance, the output environment of the British training schools appears to be one which, of the three, represents the lesser market threat. But as shall be discussed, complexities in the British training situation in fact makes the nautical education system there as problematic as either the American or the Spanish system.

The schools in these three countries, then, are confronted with unique sets of problems in adapting to the peculiarities of their market economies. Most importantly, however, these schools are differentially constrained and limited in their capacities for effective adaptation. In some instances, the school may be totally incapable of making what might appear to be an easy and optimum adjustment to a clearly understood and easily discernible market contingency.[4] Although there are numerous factors which help to limit the range of possible organisational response, the most fundamental are those imposed by the particular structural constraints under which school operations take place. As will be shown, each nautical training system is linked both to the economic realities of the market for which it is training students, *and* to distinctive systems of external control and accountability. At a general level, the most profound constraint has to do with the fact that the schools in each country operate under distinctively different sponsorships: the typical American Academy is a quasi-independent college within a state system of higher education; the Spanish schools are instruments in the hierarchy of the Spanish Ministry of Commerce; the British schools operate under the joint sponsorship of local (municipal) educational authorities and various groups in the British shipping industry. Thus school sponsorship clearly identifies the principal 'interested parties' to nautical education and constitutes the fundamental source of organisational constraint. An examination of the systems of sponsorship in each of these three countries illustrates this fact most vividly.

The American academies are four-year residential colleges which operate an eleven-month programme of training. During this time the 'Midshipmen' are given instruction directed towards preparing them for the US Coast Guard Second Mate's Examination.

The training given by the typical American academy to simulate the future real work situation is accomplished through the use of full-size training ships, usually of the dry cargo type, which are moored and maintained at the academies through the nine months during which land-based instruction is carried out. During the remaining two months of the teaching year, these ships are used to take large groups of students on a trans-ocean training cruise. The simulation is only approximate, however, inasmuch as no cargo is loaded or unloaded, the cruises are recreational as well as instructional in purpose, and the midshipmen students occupy a status which is a mix of deck-hand, student and second mate. In broad outline, navigational and marine engineering education has the following four year cycle in these schools:

TABLE 8.1   *Sequence of American Nautical Training*

1st year	2nd year	3rd year	4th year
L	S L	S L	S L

L = Land-based Training; S = Ship-board Training

It is of importance to emphasise that this way of organising the practical and theoretical aspects of nautical training in the United States is largely a function of the autonomous nature and independent structure of the American academies. Moreover, the typical American school is a component unit in a State system of higher education and as such must negotiate for financial support in a situation of competition with a variety of other State colleges and universities— and in some cases with the full range of public schools from kindergarten to graduate school. However, because the American academies are also colleges giving general education training and awarding accredited university degrees, the annual funding process does not necessarily require the schools to demonstrate either market or national need for the nautical–vocational component of their educational programmes. In this regard, the academies exhibit some of the features of all American colleges and universities including very considerable institutional autonomy and self direction with regard to programme development. Indeed, the internal allocation of available funds is largely a function of decisions made by the school itself operating only under the direction of guidelines laid down by regional college accreditation boards. In addition, while some of the academies are beginning to establish procedures for recruiting students, these have more to do with securing adequate numbers for the US maritime industry. The problem of job placement is very largely resolved through maritime labour unions which intervene between academies and the employment market. The inputs made by the consuming units—the shipping companies—either to curriculum content or numbers of students are minimal.

Due to the declining market for graduates of US maritime academies the primary problem faced by such schools is to maintain themselves as viable educational institutions. Insulated as they are from control by the US maritime industry *and* heavily dependent on state funds, the survival of these schools depends not so much on adapting to the need of the industry as it does on providing educational services for students. One might speculate that if current trends continue the large measure of curriculum autonomy and flexibility enjoyed by the American academies may well lead them to de-emphasise the nautical–vocational component of their educational programme and train students for land-based maritime careers with increased stress on vocationally transferable skills and general education.

A second variant organisation for technical nautical training is represented by the Spanish case. There are five official nautical 'Schools' in Spain and four operated under private auspices. The private schools are of little consequence in terms of numbers of students served, and in any event operate with curriculums identical to those found in the official schools. The five official schools are directed, financed, supervised and staffed by the Sub-Secretariat for the Merchant Marine, a division in the Ministry of Commerce in Madrid which has status equal to that of the Marina Armada, or Spanish Navy. Whereas the American academy enjoys a marked degree of organisational autonomy, the external structural extensions of the Spanish schools permit almost no independent internal decision-making. Subordinate as they are to the financial, administrative, examination and policy control of the hierarchy of the Ministry of Commerce, the Spanish schools are assured of a relatively constant flow of both students and finances, and a more or less continuing and stable curriculum content. This uniformity across schools in staffing, equipment and curriculum allows for virtually no flexibility within schools to adapt to locally perceived school needs.

While the structural characteristics of American academies produce external uncertainties, the opposite is found in the Spanish schools. External uncertainties are smoothed by the authority of the Ministry of Commerce hierarchy which holds the legal authority and capacity to shield the schools from the numerous external contingencies which occupy the attention of American academies. Inasmuch as the Ministry controls the curriculums, the syllabi, the staff of the schools, the rates of pay of merchant marine personnel, the production costs of merchant vessels, etc., the Ministry passes on to the school only internal uncertainties and strains. Indeed, many problems attend the rigid and inflexible curriculum structure which has been created solely for the purpose of furthering the national goal of a larger merchant marine fleet. In failing to provide occupationally transferable training for students, the Spanish system of nautical training now faces threats by both school Student Delegations and 'Professional' officer syndicates to strike the schools until the function of nautical training is readjusted so as to provide a meaningful land-based occupational role for merchant marine personnel, and to provide a graduating credential with meaningful implications for later placement in the Spanish system of social stratification. In terms of training sequence, the Spanish model is shown below:

TABLE 8.2   *Cycle of Spanish Training*

1st year	2nd year	3rd year	4th year
L	L	S	S

.... 2 years .... 400 days............

L = Land-based Training; S = Ship-board Training

Both deck and engineering students attend a land-based nautical school for a period of two years, after which they must seek temporary employment with a shipping company. Following that service they may then return to the school either to sit their Second Mate's examination, or for an additional year of classroom instruction. They have a further option of devoting the fifth year to Marina Armada training, should they at that time wish to hold a reserve officer commission in the Spanish Navy.

Hence, in Spain there is no attempt to integrate land-based training with practical training aboard ship. No effort is made to co-ordinate the students' instructional experience at school with those aboard ship. The simplicity of the line of command from the Sub-Secretariat of the Merchant Marine down to the Official Nautical Schools precludes a more complex ordering of instructional patterns and relationships to include ship companies and their employees

In sum, the structural extensions of the Spanish schools provide protection from student input and output contingencies in the twin senses that the hierarchy of authority of which the schools are but a subordinate unit control both the conditions of student entrance, and the market circumstances for their employment following the conclusion of the training process. Thus, while the Spanish ministry of Commerce assumes the responsibility for adapting to any and all external contingencies, the schools themselves are by no means free from organisational dilemmas. Without the benefit of any decision-making powers these schools must contend with the internal dissatisfactions and strains which have accompanied their rapid expansion.

In contrast to both the United States and Spain, navigators and engineers are supplied to the British Merchant Navy by no less than twenty-three separate nautical 'schools' or 'colleges'. Typically, schools occupy departmental status in municipally operated technical colleges which offer, in addition to nautical training, a wide range of other vocational instruction—electronics, building construction, printing technology and other craft training. Most students in these schools are candidates for an 'Ordinary National Certificate' in marine sciences, a nationally recognised designation of educational achievement. The closest American approximation would be a junior college 'associate degree', in a technical programme of training. There is no Spanish equivalent. Not only are the British nautical colleges in fact departments within locally supervised and controlled municipal technical colleges but, in addition, both their curriculums and finances derive from a pluralistic combination of national interest groups. These fiscal and curriculum coalitions represent the interests of the shipping industry (through the British Shipping Federation and the Merchant Navy Training Board), national *general* educational interests (through local educational authorities under the direction of the Department of Education and Science), the interests of individual shipping companies (through sponsorship of nautical students and payments to individual nautical 'colleges'); the national interest in maintaining a competitive Merchant Marine (through the Department of Trade and Industry); and the interests of the schools themselves (through the Association of Navigation Schools and the Association of Marine Engineering Schools); and finally, the interests of the seafarer himself (through the Merchant Navy and Airline Officers' Association).

The cycle of land and sea-based training is shown on next page.

An important contrast from the American and British models is found in the different streams of training for navigators as compared with engineers.

The navigating 'cadets' go directly to sea aboard a ship owned by

TABLE 8.3 *Cycle of British Training*

	1st year	2nd year	3rd year	4th year
Deck	S	L S	L S	L
Eng.	L	L	S	L S

L = Land-based Training; S = Ship-board Training

the company with which they have become employed and which is subsidising their training. The latter spend the first two years in residence at a nautical 'college' chosen by the sponsoring company. The deck cadets then alternate sea and land service for approximately three and a half years followed by six months' college training for their Second Mate's Certificate. The engineering students remain in residence at college for two years. Then they spend approximately twelve months aboard ship, then yet another year in land training. Finally an additional six months at sea before returning to college for their final examinations is undertaken.

For both navigators and engineers, however, a dual line of instruction is involved. There is a teaching faculty in the colleges and an instructional system within each shipping company—and aboard each ship—which attempts to integrate land and sea-based instruction in an effort to achieve a level of student learning acceptable to the wide range of external influences to which British schools have become accountable. Although it would be a gross oversimplification to say that the Spanish nautical schools have one master and that the American academies have none, in terms of impact upon curriculum content and school operation, it is accurate to say that the British schools have several. While the interests of *no single* interested party predominates, conflict between them is evident. Because of such complex external lines of accountability in the British nautical colleges, the curriculum which is taught is at least *partially* negotiated *at each individual school*. It is not uniform in all as in Spain; nor may it have the wide range of differences possible in the American situation. Moreover, the British system of nautical education marches a middle-line between the Spanish system, of purely 'technical' and sea-oriented education, and the general education-university degree and land-oriented training of the American academies. In Britain layer upon layer of nationally accredited certificates of educational accomplishment are issued, developed out of syllabi and curriculums which represent formally negotiated accommodations between the numerous interest groups which impinge upon these schools.

A persistent point of potential conflict over the content of the curriculum has to do with the interests of the shipping companies in vocationally specific and relevant instruction on the one hand, and the interests of the local educational authorities in more scientifically general education on the other. This conflict is sharpened by the fact that students enter British nautical colleges as a result of being recruited by the British Shipping Federation or by making an application directly to a shipping company. In either case students attend the schools as paid employees of a particular shipping company and in most cases attend a school chosen by that company. The circumstances and conditions of student entrance are so structured as to meet the manpower needs of the industry, as a whole, to fill the instructional spaces available in the nautical colleges throughout the country, while at the same time meeting the needs of the individual shipping company contracting for the sponsorship and financial support of their student/employees. There is, therefore, a component of involuntarism in nautical school attendance in Britain which is absent in the USA and in Spain. The applicant may select the work, though he may not be able to select his first choice of either employer or college. The shipping companies therefore are in a unique position to enrol their student-employees in those schools which they feel best serve their interests. These interests are in the direction of obtaining, at a minimum of cost, officers trained in an increasingly sophisticated applied maritime technology. However, the colleges are constrained by the general educational authorities from streamlining their curriculums so as to provide only technical–vocational training. These authorities, which provide the bulk of the funds to meet school-operating expenses, insist that students receive a general scientific education designed to emphasise vocationally transferable skills. The schools, dependent as they are on both sources for students and funds, must somehow adapt to the interests of both.

Required as they are to provide an extensive general scientific curriculum much in opposition to the immediate interests of the industry, the British nautical colleges compete for the support of the shipping companies by placing considerable emphasis on an additional aspect of their training programme—namely the moral socialisation of their students. Inasmuch as the British nautical schools are unable to compete with one another for the support of shipping companies on the basis of differences in curriculum, they are free to manipulate the character and quality of the residential life of their students so as to produce graduates who conform to some distinctive definition of officerhood. Thus, by enrolling their student-employees in different nautical colleges, the shipping companies exercise the choice of having their young officers trained to conform either to a military, an officer-gentleman, a business manager or loyal technician-employee model. Indeed, each model implies a differential appeal to the various shipping companies, and represents a primary method by which each college may distinguish itself from others. Why one company prefers military type officers over loyal technician employees is not necessarily the result of a rational decision-making process but, nevertheless, such preferences do in fact exist. Therefore, it is by conforming to the curricular requirements of the local educational authorities and by training a distinctive officer type for the shipping companies that the British nautical colleges adapt to the conflicting pressures imposed on them by their various sponsors. However, such diverse lines of external accountability produce considerable internal instability for these schools due to the fact that they must constantly mediate among the ever changing demands imposed upon them.

As educational institutions, maritime training schools are a general resource which can be mobilised and utilised to maximise the interests of a variety of potential beneficiaries. However, it is the form of sponsorship under which these schools operate and the lines of accountability which link them to their external environments.

Sponsorship of Spanish nautical education maximises the use of nautical schools in the national interest of expanding the Spanish Merchant Marine and enlarging its impact in the total national economy. At the same time this form of organisation minimises the use of the schools as a specific resource for individual shipping companies. More importantly, as a result of circumscribing curriculum content to that necessary for the specific work of lower rank ship's officers, such a form of organisation imposes sharp limitations on the ways in which the school may be used as a general resource by its students.

The Spanish nautical student may acquire the skills and credentials necessary to engineer or navigate a ship but almost nothing in addition.

In the typical American case, the quasi-autonomous and independent college form of sponsorship provides the student with primary access to the school as a resource. The American academies are not maintained specifically to further the interests of the sponsoring state governments or the shipping companies but to provide meaningful and useful training for the students themselves. In so doing such schools provide both general education and vocationally specific training for students, thus setting the stage for internal conflict and stress between these two competing instructional orientations.

The sponsorship of British nautical education results in the most complete range of external parties potentially interested in using maritime colleges as a resource. The pluralistic dependence of such schools is such that the interests of local and national educational authorities and of the shipping industry, in both its collective and individual representations, have combined to produce distinctive curriculum and internal school administrative structures.

In sum, the Spanish schools, as resources, are reserved overwhelmingly for utilisation by their single sponsoring agent—the Ministry of Commerce. Consequently, technical education predominates to the total exclusion of general education. The quasi-independent American academies by way of contrast are resources given over for utilisation primarily by students with little concern for the interests of external parties. Here the schools wage internal debate over the issue of providing general versus technical training for students.

Finally, the British nautical schools are open systems in which curriculum content and school operations are the result of determinations made almost entirely by the various parties external to the schools themselves. As a result the lines of conflict between general and vocational education are thinly visible within the schools but sharply drawn between the external parties which are competing for more exclusive access to the schools as resources.

These cross-national comparisons pinpoint a persistent problem concerning the double-function of maritime education for students. Double-function refers to the fact that such schools are, on the one hand, constrained to equip students to become ships' officers with highly specialised skills and knowledge and, are, on the other hand, pressed to offer both educational experience and academic credential which will allow the seafarer to come ashore and enter into the land-based world of work in a job which bears some relation to the four years or more of specialised training he has undergone. Indeed, while nautical students enter a highly specialised and temporary career as a seafarer there is increasing expectation that their education will give them both occupational skills and insignia of social rank which they may carry into the society of landsmen after having 'swallowed the anchor'.

Again, the prevailing mode of maritime school sponsorship and external accountability are important determinants of just how schools adapt to this double-function process. In the Spanish case nautical training is restricted in its applicability to shipboard service with little carry over to re-entry into land-based society. The graduates of these schools comprise an important resource implementing the attainment of national economic goals towards which school organisation is aimed. Nautical education, and the sea-based employment opportunities to which it is addressed, constitutes an expanding source of income for young men in Spain, a country now entering seriously into industrialisation and international trade. The dilemma created, however, is that the pursuit of collective economic success in the merchant marine field may effectively exclude attention to the legitimate post-seafaring occupational and social rank interests of students.[5] In such cases as Spain the immediate market for seafarers is an expanding and temporarily lucrative one. But re-entrance into the landed occupational opportunity structure and system of social ranking is not enabled by the content of education permitted by the sponsorship structure of the Spanish nautical schools. Paradoxically, it is only after some measure of success has been achieved in the collective national purposes of nautical education that questions of post-sea employment and later social class position become problematical.

Britain, by way of contrast, represents an advanced stage of a working accommodation between the double-functions of nautical education for students. This is brought about by its complex system of sponsorship, its numerous external lines of accountability, and their accompanying cumbersome attempt to integrate land relevant training with seafaring training. The product is a curriculum with the most complex mix of technical training 'for the job', later occupational placement through more advanced 'scientific' training, and subsequent social class placement through the award of a nationally recognised credential of intellectual accomplishment placing the recipient in the company of workers who are pursuing vocationally specific employment in spheres other than seafaring.

In the American academies, the college form of sponsorship leads to yet another mix of training. The board extension of publicly supported general education in the United States is reflected in the now firmly established—and sharply distinguished—dual curriculums found in these schools. One aims to equip the midshipmen to carry out the special responsibilities which fall upon the shoulders of the employees of ocean-going ships. The other intends to designate the student as a university graduate, signified by a credential announcing his claims to a generalised social rank equal to that of all other university baccalaureate graduates. The fact of a declining national market for deck and engineering officers moves the typical American academy to seek for new markets into which to send their graduates, and to try to equip them with alternate vocational skills to make them otherwise employable.

There is, therefore, in the British system of nautical education a strong set of structural components serving to legitimise the seafarer's anticipated departure from his sea-going career and his re-entry into *roughly* the same social status he might otherwise have occupied had he never gone to sea. In the American case, there is a very strong upward mobility element in the training offered, aimed towards equipping the student for re-entry to the landed social system at a significantly higher in the scheme of things than he might have found himself had he not gone to sea. But Spain, with its expanding merchant marine industry, cannot help but be confronted with the fact that such expansion could lead to even sharper conflicts between the double-function of nautical education: service aboard ships on the one hand, and social status on land on the other.

REFERENCES

1. See especially Peter H. Fricke, 'The Social Organisation of the Crews of British Dry-Cargo Merchant Ships: A Study of the Organization and Environment of an Occupation' (Ph.D. Dissertation, University of Durham, 1972); Warren H. Hopwood, 'Preparing to be a Merchant Navy Officer: A Study in Occupational Socialisation' (M. Ed. Dissertation, University of Bristol, 1971); C. H. Milsom, *Guide to the Merchant Navy*. Brown, Son & Ferguson, Ltd., Glasgow, 1968; Stephen A. Richardson, 'Organizational Contrasts on British and American Ships', *Administrative Science Quarterly*, Vol. I, 1956, pp. 168–206.
2. This chapter is written as if the worlds of nautical education in the three countries are completely uniform school to school. Like most other worlds they are not. The patterns of training, and influences upon schools described here, are the dominant and

macro-patterns and influences in each country. Some of the important extensions of the arguments presented here, and an examination of some of the important variations, will be discussed in a forthcoming monograph by the authors of this chapter, entitled, *Society, Organization and Technical Education: A Cross-National Study of Merchant Marine Training.*

3. The most careful assessment is in The Right Honourable the Viscount Rochdale, *Committee of Inquiry into Shipping: Report.* Her Majesty's Stationery Office, London, 1970.

4. Central to open-system theory is the view that organisations make those adaptations to conditions in their external environment which will be maximising for the goals of the organisation. See for example, Daniel Katz and Robert L. Kohn, *The Social Psychology of Organizations.* John Wiley and Sons, New York, 1966; Paul R. Lawrence and Jay W. Lorsch, *Organisation and Environment.* Richard D. Irwin, Inc.; Homewood, 1967; *Readings in Organization Theory—Open-System Approaches.* John G. Maurer (ed.), Random House, New York, 1971; James D. Thompson, *Organizations in Action.* McGraw-Hill, New York, 1967. Such a view rests upon the assumption that autonomy and independence are maximising strategies for organisations, a key aspect of which is the pursuit of goals which are internally generated. A limitation of this perspective is the fact that organisations may often be constrained to pursue goals imposed upon them by external agents. As we shall argue, sponsorship structures are central both to determining organisational goals and limiting adaptive capabilities.

5. This problem has been recently explored in J. M. M. Hill, *The Seafaring Career*, The Tavistock Institute of Human Relations, London, 1972.

Nine · Family and Community: The Environment of the Ships' Officer

PETER H. FRICKE

INTRODUCTION

This paper examines the problems of the seafarer and his family, and the subsequent effect on attitudes to seafaring. The information is based upon the responses of seafarers over twenty years of age in the British Merchant Navy to a questionnaire survey and is also drawn from interviews. The sample has been taken from mature seafarers only in order to provide a balance between the married and single seafarers so that an analysis of comparable factors can be achieved.

TABLE 9.1   *Structure of sample: the response of seafarers over 20 years of age (Questionnaire Survey)*

	Married: N	Single N	Married (per cent)
Deck officers	26	24	52
Engineer officers	33	47	41
Total N	59	71	47

THE HOME BACKGROUND OF SEAFARERS: OFFICERS

Deck officers came from families which had a significantly different socio-economic background to those of engineer officers. However, no significant difference in family size occurred between the two groups (2.2 children in the engineer officers' families; 2.3 in the deck officers'). The difference within the groups lay between those who said they wished to make the sea their career or who had relatives at sea.

The families of those officers who had relatives at sea or intended to make the sea their career were significantly larger and contained a higher proportion of female siblings than the national average (1.65 versus 1.17).[1]

132

The parents of those officers who intended making the sea their career also differed significantly from those of the sample as a whole. The officer who wished to make the sea his career was more than twice as likely to have come from a single-parent family than an officer who intended leaving the sea, since one in three career officers came from a single parent home, while the ratio was one in five in the whole sample.

TABLE 9.2 *Parents in the home: officers.*

		Main sample	Career at sea	Relatives at sea
		%	%	%
Deck officers:	One parent	18	37	42
	Two parents	82	63	58
	N =	50	24	26
Engineer officers:	One parent	18	30	18
	Two parents	82	70	82
	N =	80	20	46

These factors of the larger, female-dominated sibling group and the high proportion of single-parent families among the officers who intend to make the sea their career are most important, since they indicate that the ship provides an area of masculine security. In this sense these men are electing to stay at sea because it offers a secure base for other social activity and for social satisfactions which would be missing ashore. As we have noted elsewhere,[2] the deck officer cannot easily transfer his skills to a shore job; therefore, in addition to the group with an inadequate background, there are those officers who cannot find shore employment. Consequently, the job satisfaction levels of career deck officers is less than that of engineer officers who can obtain work ashore relatively easily and only stay at sea if they really wish to.[3]

These scales also indicate that being married does not affect the career of a seafarer to the extent suggested by many shipping companies. Marriage is a watershed in any man's life, but in the sample the key issues were whether the man could obtain, keep and enjoy work ashore. Many personnel officers in shipping companies forget that the age-group of marriage of a ship's officer coincides with the age-range in which he decides, like most young professional

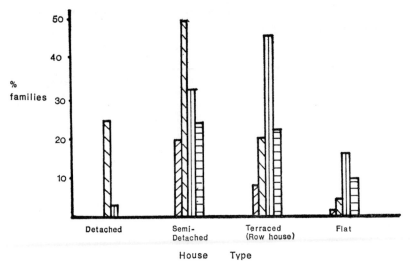

TABLE 9.3A *Parents' homes*

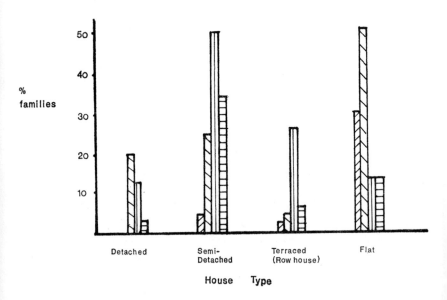

TABLE 9.3B *Officers' homes.*

employees,[4] what his future career requires. As we shall see, once the career choice has been finalised, the choice of wife will fit it.

In the choice of homes, significant differences appeared between deck and engineer officers' houses and between the houses of their parents (see Table 9.3). This latter, of course, reflects the occupational patterns. The pattern of home ownership of the seafarers themselves reflects their life styles. The majority of young deck officers (51 per cent) lived in flats, since this form of housing was most convenient as wives were working and families had not been yet started. When houses were bought, they mirrored the salary levels of the deck officers and were at the upper end of the parents' scale of housing. On the other hand, the engineer officers tended to marry and start a family almost immediately. Few of their wives worked for long after marriage and a noticeable improvement in housing is evident.

The level of rented accommodation has declined slightly (57 per cent of parents rent their homes against 55 per cent of the engineer officers), but the proportion of terraced houses has declined from 48 per cent (parents) to 25 per cent (engineer officers). This group makes extensive use of council housing (30 per cent) and housing co-operatives (10 per cent); the rest of the housing is obtained through private landlords. Only 36 per cent of the deck officers rent their houses, and just one man in the sample (2 per cent) lived in council property (a flat provided for his wife who was a school-teacher). The one-third who rented accommodation were largely in the younger age group (21–25 years) and the majority of this rented accommodation was flats.

The Wives of Officers

[Seafaring] is a hell of a life for a married man with a family [and] more so for those at home. It's the wives that deserve all the praise, being father and mother, while there [sic] husbands are away at least 9 months of the year.[5]

As a bachelor a seafarer ashore has plenty of money and freedom to do as he pleases. On leave, he is in the situation of having free time for approximately three months every year. The majority of these leave periods will be spent at his parents' home or holidaying with them, and his future wife will probably be a local girl (69 per cent) and come from a similar socio-economic background as the seafarer. Table 4 shows the occupations of the wives of seafarers in the sample before marriage.

It is apparent that the deck officers' wives have white-collar, middle-class occupations, and that over one-third are, like their husbands, quasi-professionals.[6] Each of these women has worked for her living, unlike the wives of engineer officers, of whom 9 per cent had not worked either because they married when very young or were unable to find employment. 42 per cent of the engineers' wives

TABLE 9.4 *The jobs of officers' wives before marriage.*

	Deck officers' wives	Engineer officers' wives	All wives
Manual	0	33%	19%
Skilled	0	9%	5%
Clerical	65%	48%	56%
Professional	35%	0%	15%
No job	0%	9%	5%
Total (%)	100%	99%	100%
N =	26	33	59

had held manual or skilled jobs, mostly in the service industries (9 wives), although some had worked on assembly lines and in factories (5 wives). Those wives of engineer officers who had held clerical posts had typically worked as file clerks, comptometer operators, telephonists or invoice clerks.

Although our sample is very limited, we can say that the choice of wife lies within the socio-economic grouping of the officer's family. Moreover, as we shall find in our discussion of Table 9A, 62 per cent of deck officers' wives and 68 per cent of engineer officers' wives live within ten miles of the seafarer's parents' home. Since 46 per cent of the mates and 36 per cent of the engineers came from non-seafaring areas of Britain, many of these wives lived in areas where the problems of the seafarer's family were rarely encountered. If the wife was able to continue working after marriage, the possibility of her husband's saying that he would stay at sea as a career increased by 27 per cent in the case of deck officers and 20 per cent in the case of engineer officers.

In both cases the wives of men who seek a career at sea tend to come from occupations at the 'higher' end of the occupational scale. Thus, the wives in quasi-professional occupations are more

TABLE 9.5A *The jobs of officers' wives after marriage.*

	Deck officers' wives	Engineer officers' wives	All wives
Manual	0	3%	2%
Skilled	0	9%	5%
Clerical	42%	24%	32%
Professional	27%	0	12%
No job	31%	64%	49%
Total (%)	100%	100%	100%
N =	26	33	59

TABLE 9.5B *The jobs of career officers' wives after marriage*

	Deck officers' wives	Engineer officers' wives	All wives
Manual	0	0	0
Skilled	0	0	0
Clerical	44%	48%	42%
Professional	33%	0	18%
No job	23%	52%	40%
Total	100%	100%	100%
N =	18	15	33

likely to be married to a career deck officer, and a girl who has done clerical work is more apt to marry a career engineer officer than one who has worked in a factory.

Two factors are at play in this system of choice. The first is that the seafarer tends to be socially mobile and will seek a wife who can be likewise in her own socio-economic strata. A girl who is a quasi-professional will have been through a training and socialisation process similar to that of the deck officer and is therefore more independent than other women of the same socio-economic group. This also holds true of the office worker from a 'blue-collar' back-ground. As Lockwood observed in his study of clerks,[7] the work in an office has always been deemed superior to that in a factory, and there is evidence that the engineer officer recognises this and chooses his wife accordingly. If he is socially mobile and more likely to stay at sea some time, he will tend to marry a girl who can also be mobile or has a better job in the terms of their mutual working-class background.

The second factor is that the seafarer is aware that his wife must be capable of standing on her own feet and running a home and family by herself. As one Master put the problem:

> When you are a young man you have a lot of money to spend, mostly on yourself. Then you get a Second Mate's job and get married. From then on you don't have the slightest idea where the money goes. If you pay all the bills you find yourself in the position of worrying about the mail, so your wife pays them all. Your balance in the ship [money left after the allotment note has been paid] is the only money you have control over to convert into capital. Since most young mates leave their full allotment allowance [90 per cent of the seafarer's basic wage] to their wives, I'm sure that the only reason mothers-in-law allow their daughters to marry seamen is that the daughter can lead an independent life financed from a long way away.[8]

The wife of the career seaman must be able to manage her own life, and the choice of a wife who has had experiences outside the normal routine of the house ensures that she is better equipped to cope with the problems created by an absent husband.

In the choice of his wife the seafarer is aided by his relative wealth as a bachelor and by his exposure to girls at ships' parties[9] and the places and events he goes to on leave. As we mentioned earlier, the seafarer has usually made his choice of career before his choice of marriage partner, and no significant difference shows up between single men who chose to make the sea their career and married men other than the fact of marriage and a preference on the part of single men for longer voyages.

When the married officer is at home on leave, a significant difference does appear between deck and engineer officers concerning the persons with whom his wife and he associate in their leisure time. This disparity is partially due to socio-economic background and partly because the majority of deck officers' wives continue to work until they start a family and frequently return to work when the children are in school.

TABLE 9.6 *Persons with whom the officer and his wife spend leisure time together during leave periods*

	Deck officer	Engineer officer	All
Shipmates	7%	18%	13%
Neighbours	7%	15%	12%
Relatives	27%	43%	36%
Wife's friends	31%	24%	27%
Officer's friends	27%	0	13%
Total (%)	99%	100%	101%
N =	26	33	59

As we can see in Table 9.6, visits to relatives occupy a smaller proportion of leisure time for mates than for engineers, and a greater amount of time is spent with the wife's friends (mostly from her place of work) and non-seafaring friends of the deck officer. The engineer officer and his wife, on the other hand, spend more time with friends who are seafarers and with neighbours and relatives. These last reflect the values of the working-class community and the visiting patterns expected within it.[10]

The Officer's Wife Within The Community

While her husband is at sea, the officer's wife has to rely on her own resources for her social life. Since the socio-economic backgrounds of officers and their wives are similar, their social relationships show this. Although a third of the visitors to the seafarer's home are

TABLE 9.7 *Wife's female visitors when husband is at sea*

	Deck officer's wife	Engineer officer's wife
Friend	49%	34%
Relative	35%	33%
Neighbour	17%	32%
Total (%)	101%	99%
N =	26	33

relatives in the case of deck and engineer officers, community and housing patterns create significant differences between the other categories of visitor. The engineer officer's wife interacts with her neighbours to a larger extent than the deck officer's wife. The latter interacts more with friends who are not neighbours and who travel

TABLE 9.8 *Distance travelled by visitor to officer's wife (in minutes)*

	Deck officers' wives	Engineer officers' wives
0–7 minutes	21%	44%
8–11 minutes	14%	7%
12–15 minutes	10%	12%
More than 16 minutes	55%	37%
Total (%)	100%	100%

TABLE 9.9A *Distance of the married seafarer's immediate family* from his home (distance in miles: per cent of immediate family)*

	Deck officer	Engineer officer
0–2 miles	30%	21%
3–5 miles	20%	32%
6–10 miles	12%	15%
11–50 miles	20%	8%
More than 51 miles	17%	24%
Total (%)	99%	100%
N =	26	33

* Immediate family = parents and siblings

some distance to visit. Whereas 35 per cent of all the visitors to deck officers' wives live within easy walking or travelling distance (that is, an eleven-minute journey), 51 per cent of the visitors to engineer officers' wives live within that distance, and 44 per cent live within five minutes. As a result, the engineer's wife is embedded in the structure of her community to a greater extent than the white-collar deck officer's wife.

This pattern repeats itself within the families of the seafarer and his wife. Since the support needed by the wife when the husband is away is usually provided by her mother, the residence pattern of the seafarer is matrilocal, although it must be stated that the seafarer's immediate family is also normally resident within the area.

TABLE 9.9B *Distance of the immediate family* of the seafarer's wife from her home (distance in miles: per cent of immediate family)*

	Deck Officer	Engineer Officer
0–2 miles	40%	54%
3–5 miles	30%	12%
6–10 miles	4%	5%
11–50 miles	4%	19%
More than 51 miles	23%	9%
Total (%)	101%	100%
$N =$	26	33

* Immediate family = parents and siblings.

TABLE 9.9C *Distance of the immediate family* of the career seafarer's wife from her home*

	Deck officer's wife	Engineer officer's wife
0–2 miles	44%	59%
3–5 miles	39%	20%
6–10 miles	6%	7%
More than 51 miles	11%	7%
Total (%)	100%	100%
$N =$	18	15

* Immediate family = parents and siblings.

The officer who decides to make the sea his career is even more apt to select a home close to his wife's parents, and this reflects itself in a significant difference in the home location between career and non-career officers (Tables 9.9B and 9.9C).

TABLE 9.10A *Frequency with which an officer's wife sees her relatives**

	Deck officers' wives	Engineer officers' wives
Every day	62%	76%
Twice a week	19%	12%
Monthly ·	12%	9%
Less frequently	8%	3%
Total (%)	101%	100%
N =	26	33

* Relatives = parents and siblings.

TABLE 9.10B *Frequency with which a career officer's wife sees her relatives**.

	Deck officers' wives	Engineer officers' wives
Every day	72%	82%
Twice a week	22%	12%
Monthly	6%	6%
Less frequently	0	0
Total (%)	100%	100%
N =	18	15

* Relatives = parents and siblings.

The matrilocal feature of the residence of officers and wives is apparent in the patterns of visiting between the wife and her relatives. This pattern is shown in Tables 9.10A and 9.10B and is intensified when the officer is making the sea his career. Close proximity to her family's home in the case of the engineer's wife (also see Tables 9.8 and 9.9B) is demonstrated in the higher level of daily visits, but these are more frequent than those recorded, for example, in Young and Willmott[11] for married daughters. The deck officer's wife also has a higher frequency of interaction with her family than a middle-class married daughter would normally have,[12] and visits are increased during periods in which there are young children or illness in the house.

TABLE 9.11A *Seafarers' wives with friends who are other seafarers' wives (whole sample)*

	Deck officers' wives	Engineer officers' wives
1 or 2 friends	50%	43%
Several friends	19%	21%
No seafarers' wives as friends	31%	36%
Total (%)	100%	100%
$N =$	26	33

TABLE 9.11B *Career seafarers' wives with friends who are other seafarers' wives*

	Deck officers' wives	Engineer officers' wives
1 or 2 friends	55%	47%
Several friends	23%	33%
No seafarers' wives as friends	22%	20%
Total (%)	100%	100%
$N =$	18	15

Seafarers' wives know of one another within a community and frequently interact. Again, the wives of career officers knew a higher proportion of other seafarers' families than the wives of non-career officers. These women meet through mutual friends rather than through the seafarer's work friendships and frequently help one another during leave periods or school holidays.

I met Monica at a night class we were taking at the Tech. two years ago, and we have been firm friends ever since. When Bob and John, her husband, are away we go to the cinema or a concert together once a week, and went to the Ideal Home Exhibition as well last year. My mother looks after the children and tries to understand what it's like without Bob home, but Monica is in the same boat so to speak as myself and I don't have to explain why I'm blue after four weeks and no letter. She can pull the efficiency of the so-called postal service apart much more concisely than me.[13]

TABLE 9.12A *Attitudes of officers' wives to husband's seagoing (whole sample)*

	Deck officers' wives	Engineer officers' wives
Non-committal	8%	12%
Prefers him home	46%	33%
Does not like it	27%	43%
Extreme dislike	19%	12%
Total (%)	100%	100%
$N =$	26	33

TABLE 9.12B *Attitudes of officers' wives to husband's seagoing (career sample)*

	Deck officers' wives	Engineer officers' wives
Non-committal	11%	20%
Prefers him home	50%	33%
Does not like it	28%	33%
Extreme dislike	11%	13%
Total %	100%	99%
$N =$	18	15

Tables 9.12A and 9.12B show the extent to which there is recognition of the concern of the officer's wife about his work at sea. Many wives obviously dislike it, since it takes her husband away from home. The small sample, however, does not permit a test of significance of the data, and trends shown must be interpreted with caution, as these are the husbands' perceptions of the wives' attitudes.

To summarise, the seafarer's wife reflects his attitudes towards a career at sea in her occupation and independence. The choice of her location, her patterns of visitors and visiting, and her friends also parallel the choice of the seafarer in his career.

DISCUSSION

The patterning of family and community we have summarised above can be considered as an adaptation of normal social life, as defined by landsmen, to meet the problems encountered by the seafarer. It is from this coping with the environment of seafaring as an occupation that we will discuss the seafarer's family.

Lawrence and Lorsch[14] have argued that in complex societies there are opposing social forces. The first of these, differentiation, is a function of the division of labour, in that skills or an occupation become highly specialised and hence differentiated from other skills or occupations. The second force is that of integration since any social system must operate as a whole, by its very definition. These two forces must therefore find an equilibrium if a social system, such as a community or occupation, is to operate and continue to operate. There are obviously many factors, not least the economic and technological aspects, which influence this equilibrium. In any form of social organisation a balance must be struck between those factors which lead to differentiation and those which lead to integration. Barth has argued that this interconnection of life-experience is transactional and reciprocal,[15] and similar arguments have been advanced by Behrend and Baldamus[16] with regard to the purely industrial aspects of life experience.

For the seafarer the initial differentiation is that posed by the environment of his work; physical separation from society ashore and working in a mobile community set the seafarer apart from landsmen of the same age and socio-economic characteristics. Further differentiation occurs on the ship between individuals with different skills, e.g. deckhands and cooks, and with different forms of working day.[17] Integration into this shipboard community requires the acceptance of the culture and behaviour associated with seafaring; it involves the identification of self with other seafarers and the acknowledgement of common social norms and goals. Thus emphasis upon the work-group by the seafarer further increases the differentiation between seafaring and life ashore. Consequently there are few integrating devices for linking the merchant seafarer with society ashore, although these have increased with changes in technology, e.g. the installation and availability of domestic radio and television on ships. The most important link is that with the family and the seafarer's own community in which he will spend most of his holiday periods. It is for this reason that the distinctions between the socio-economic background of seafarers; between the seafarers' experiences of family life; between career and non-career attitudes to seafaring; and finally the social needs, must be drawn. In resolving these problems in his social environment, the career officer is able to approach his work on the ship with a firm commitment.

As we have noted, deck officers or mates are drawn from a predominantly lower middle class socio-economic background. Their choice of wife also reflects this background, as shown by the white-collar and quasi-professional occupations of wives before marriage (Table 9.4). In addition the housing patterns of the parents of deck officers reflect this (Table 9.3) since 70 per cent of these families own their own homes and the housing stock is of good quality. In contrast to this the engineer officer by and large is drawn from the skilled working class. Again this is reflected in his choice of wife (Table 9.4) and in his parents' housing, 58 per cent of which is rented (Table 9.3) and of poorer quality relative to the deck officers' homes. The differentiation on board the ship due to these socio-economic inequalities is largely overcome by integration through the social structure of each rank and status. However, this integration rarely extends to the community ashore, since the differing backgrounds of the seafarers militate against it. Not only are the mates and engineer officers drawn from different parts of the community, but their experience of their communities is different. The majority of engineer officers in the sample are from large ship-building towns or cities and have served a five-year apprenticeship in an engineering works or shipyard. Their seafaring career thus started at the age of 21 or 22 years; much older than the mates who normally commence their apprenticeship at sea between the ages of 16 and 18 years. The mates, or deck officers, moreover, are recruited from smaller towns and rural areas, and go to sea immediately after leaving school in 81 per cent of the cases.

The reasons for going to sea, therefore, are due to employment opportunity, for travel or adventure and for the entrant to have the opportunity to leave home/'spread his wings'. Of these three motivations, it is the latter that concerns us most since it implies a rejection of the seafarer's home environment, and thus a lack of integration with it. This weakening of ties, and conversely a move away from deprivation in the home environment, leads to a higher level of integration into the community of the ship. Thus the significantly higher proportion of seafarers who are from single parent families (see Table 2) and who choose the sea as a career can be seen as choosing between communities. In this case the shore community is threatening to the self identity of the seafarer, while the shipboard community is not.[18]

In our society the majority of males over the age of 28 are married. This is true of seafarers as well, but our sample does not reflect this because the average age of all the officers interviewed is 28.7 years, and the majority of engineer officers spend only three years or less at sea. For those seafarers who do not wish to make the sea their life's work the time of marriage is a suitable time to leave the shipping industry. Those men who wish to stay at sea must therefore decide whether to reinforce their links with shore society through marriage, or whether to remain single and slowly move away from permanent contacts with a community ashore. Since mates and engineers who wished to remain at sea and were married were not significantly different on scores of job satisfaction and work attitudes from those who were single and intended staying at sea, it can be said that the choice of wife and family is one which is weighed in terms of a career.

That the need, to choose wives who are able to manage their households effectively and singlehandedly, is perceived by seafarers is well documented.[19] That the seafarer chooses his wife for her independence and community links, is shown in Tables 9.4, 9.5 and 9.6. The most noteworthy point is that the wife provides the vicarious link with society ashore for the married officer through the provision of a home and a network of friends. However, if there are children involved, what was once a very independent life for the wife becomes highly restricted and consequently there must be a dependence by her upon friends and neighbours to provide the necessary social support for her role as mother. It is at this period of family life that many seafarers, who are career-oriented, are pressed by their wives and families to return to life ashore. The pressure is less on engineers because they feel that they are socially mobile, and their wives are reluctant to forego the gain in status. It is in this context that Tables 9.7 to 9.11 are important. Where the wife has a highly integrated place within the kinship circle and within the community as a whole, she is able to cope with the problems of the single-parent family.

This concept of seeking a compromise in terms of occupational and communal norms provides an insight into the manner in which the seafarer lives. It must be emphasised, however, that the compromise is a highly personal, albeit social, transaction and many other variables play a part in the decision to stay at sea.

CONCLUSION

When the ship's officer intends making the sea his career, he must consider the social environment of his family. If we subsume the arguments of Lawrence and Lorsch concerning organisational environments[20] to the relationship of the seafarer to his family, we can argue that his occupation and the length of time spent at sea provide the major force for differentiation within the family.

The married seafarer to a greater extent, and the single man to a lesser one, must find means of integrating their life at sea into that of their family network ashore. The integration can take several forms. The seafarer can reject family life ashore and seek to integrate himself fully into the life at sea. This form of integration would be the pattern of socialisation to be expected if we accept Goffman's concept of socialisation into the ship-as-total-institution. Another form of integration would be abandoning life at sea and accepting the normal patterns of family life ashore. This form would presuppose the incompatibility of seafaring with family life. A third form, and it would appear to be the most common, is the search for a suitable accommodation of both family and occupational needs.

As we have seen, for the ship's officer, both his choice of wife and the locale of his home influence the possibility of making the sea his career. A wife who can enjoy the support of kinfolk and is used to a measure of independence in her day-to-day family life will allow the seafarer to remain in his occupation with an easier mind because he has been able to integrate family and occupation in a way which does not create a need to choose only one or the other. However, this accommodation of needs is only suitable in a relatively stable social environment, since it presupposes a pattern of voyages and job satisfaction which allows a family to function successfully.

REFERENCES

1. A. F. Sillitoe, *Britain in Figures*, Penguin, Harmondsworth, 1971, p. 18.
2. P. H. Fricke, The Social Structure of the Crews of British Dry-Cargo Merchant Ships, University of Durham, unpublished Ph.D. thesis. Chapter 4, 1971. Also see J. M. M. Hill, *The Seafaring Career*, Tavistock Institute for Human Relations, London, 1972.
3. P. H. Fricke, 1971, Chapter 7; especially Table 7.5.
4. Cf. K. Prandy, *Professional Employees*, Faber and Faber, London, 1965.
5. Seafarers in the sample were invited to keep a diary of their daily activities. This citation is from a diary kept by a Catering Officer on a bulk-carrier.
6. 'Professionals' in the sample were teachers, nurses, therapists and a chemist. With the exception of one, all worked in a setting characterised by Goffman as a total institution. Since they are professional employees, like the ship's officers, and are not of the recognised professions (law, for example), the term 'quasi-professional' is used to describe them.
7. D. Lockwood, *The Blackcoated Worker*, Allen & Unwin, London, 1958.
8. Diary of the Master of a bulk-carrier.
9. Ships' parties are organised, usually for the officers only, to provide a social break in the routine of a voyage. If an officer has a girl friend in a port, she will be asked to invite a dozen or so of her female friends to a party on the ship. If there are no such contacts, an officer will be delegated the task of telephoning a women's hostel attached to a hospital or college to extend an invitation to anyone who wishes to come to a party. Other social contacts are made through the hostesses at the clubs run by the Missions to Seamen or the Stella Maris.
10. M. Young, and P. Willmott, *Family and Kinship in East London* Routledge & Kegan Paul, London, 1957, Chapter 7.
11. M. Young, and P. Willmott, 1957, Chapter 5.
12. C. Rosser and C. Harris, *The Family and Social Change*, Routledge & Kegan Paul, London, 1965.
13. Interview with Second Engineer Officer's wife.
14. P. R. Lawrence and J. W. Lorsch, *Organisation and Environment*,

Richard D. Irwin, Inc. Homewood, Illinois, 1969, esp. pp. 8–20. Lawrence and Lorsch consider the state of differentiation to be the difference in cognitive and emotional orientation between members of separate functional parts of an organisation. Integration can be defined as the state of collaboration which exists between members of an organisation who are required to achieve unity of effort in attaining the goals of the environment. See also P. H. Fricke, 'The Social Role of the Naval Architect', *Shipping World and Shipbuilder*, May 1971.

15. F. Barth, *Models of Social Organization: Occasional Paper No. 23*, Royal Anthropological Institute, London, 1966, pp. 3–4.

16. H. Behrend, 'The Effort Bargain', in *Industrial and Labor Relations Review*, Vol. 10, No. 4, 1957, pp. 503–575; and W. Baldamus, 'Types of Work and Motivation', in *British Journal of Sociology*, 1951, Vol. 2.

17. For a full discussion of the social organisation of the ship see P. H. Fricke, (1972), or V. Aubert and O. Arner, (1958), 'On the Social Structure of the Ship', in *Acta Sociologica*, Vol. 3; pp. 200–19.

18. See P. H. Fricke, (1972) esp. chapter 5; and Gronseth, E. and Tiller, P. (1958), 'Father Absence in Sailor Families and its Impact upon the Personality Development and later Social Adjustment of the Children', *Nordiske Psykologi*, Monograph Series No. 9; Oslo. By single-parent families we mean those families whose father is absent for at least eight months in every year.

19. E. Gronseth, *Reactions of Seamen's Wives to Frustrations resulting from the Absence of Their Husbands*, Institute for Social Research, Oslo, 1959; J. M. M. Hill, (1972) op. cit; G. W. Horobin, (1957) 'Community and Occupation in the Hull Fishing Industry' in *British Journal of Sociology*, Vol. 8, No. 4, pp. 345–349; C. A. Pearlman, (1970), 'Separation Reactions of Married Women' in *American Journal of Psychiatry*, No. 126; G. Stiles, (1972a), 'Fishermen, Wives and Radios', in R. Andersen, and C. Wadel (eds), *North Atlantic Fishermen*.

20. Lawrence and Lorsch (1969) op. cit.

Bibliography

Andersen, R. (1972), 'Hunt and Deceive: Information Management in Newfoundland Deep-sea Trawler Fishing'. in Andersen, R., and Wadel, C. (eds.): *North Atlantic Fishermen*, Memorial University Press, St. John's, Newfoundland.

Andersen, R., and Wadel, C. (eds.) (1972), *North Atlantic Fishermen*, Memorial University Press, St. John's, Newfoundland.

Arner, O. (1961), Skipet og Sjomannen, Oslo (Mimeo.).

Aubert, V., and Arner, O. (1958–9), 'On the Social Structure of the Ship', *Acta Sociologica*, No. 3.

Aubert, V., and Arner, O. (1962), *The Ship as a Social System*, Oslo (Mimeo.).

Aubert, V., and Arner, O. (1969), 'Work and its Structural Setting', in Burns, T. (ed.), *Industrial Man*, Penguin Books, Harmondsworth.

Banfield, E. C. (1958), *The Moral Basis of a Backward Society*, Free Press, Glencoe, Ill.

Barberis, C. (1965), *Sociologia Rurale*, Universita, Bologna.

Barnett, C. (1969), *Governing Elites: Studies in Training & Selection*, Oxford University Press, New York.

Barth, F. (1966), *Models of Social Organization: Occasional Paper No. 23*, Royal Anthropological Institute, London.

Benjamin, R. (1970), 'L'Univers des Marins', *Recherche Sociale*, No. 27.

Black, W. (1960), 'The Labrador Floater Cod Fishery', *Annals of the Association of American Geographers*, Vol. 50, No. 3; pp. 267–91.

Bowalby, J. (1963), 'Pathological Mourning & Childhood Mourning', *Journal of American Psychoanalytical Association*, No. 11.

Braithewaite, R. B. (1960), *Scientific Explanation*, Harper & Row, London.

Brassey, T. (1877), *British Seamen*, Longmans, Green & Co., London.

Brim, O. G., and Wheeler, S. (1966), *Socialization after Childhood*, John Wiley & Sons, New York.

Bureau International du Travail (1952), *Les Conditions de Travail dans l'Industrie de la Peche*, Geneve.

Bureau International du Travail (1958), *Les Conditions de Travail des Pecheurs*, Geneve.

Burns, N. M. and Kimura, D. (1963), 'Isolation and Sensory Deprivation', in Burns, N. M. (ed.), *Unusual Environments and Human Behaviour*, Free Press, Glencoe, Ill.

Chance, N. A. (1968), 'Implications of Environmental Stress: Strategies of Developmental Change in the North', *Archives of Environmental Health*, Vol. 17.

Cheeseman, F. (1957), *Report of the South Coast Commission*, Government of Newfoundland and Labrador, St. John's, Newfoundland.

Chiaramonte, L. (1970), *Craftsman-Client Contracts: Interpersonal Relations in a Newfoundland Fishing Community*, Memorial University Press, St. John's, Newfoundland.

Chodoff, P. (1970), 'The German Concentration Camp as a Psychological Stress', *Archives of General Psychiatry*, Vol. 22, pp. 78–87.

Ciuffa, E. (1953), *La Cooperazione Peschereccia in Italia*, Roma.

Clemmer, D. (1958), *The Prison Community*, Holt, Rinehart & Winston, New York.

Report of Her Majesty's Commissioners of Inquiry into the Condition of the Crofters and Cottars in the Highlands and Islands of Scotland, Vol. II (1884), HMSO, Edinburgh.

Committee of Enquiry into Shipping (The Rochdale Report) (Com. 4337), (1970), HMSO, London.

Final Report of the Committee of Inquiry into Trawler Safety (The Holland–Martin Report) (1969), HMSO, London.

Copes, P. (1969). *The Role of the Fishing Industry in the Economic Development of Newfoundland*, Department of Economics and Commerce, Simon Fraser University, Discovery Paper No. 69–3–3, Burnaby, British Columbia.

Cressey, D. R. (ed.) (1961), *The Prison*, Holt, Rinehart and Winston, New York.

H.M. Customs and Excise, 'Letter Books, Collector to Board, 1791 et seq.', MSS Records of H.M. Customs and Excise, Customs House, Lerwick.

H.M. Customs and Excise, 'Register of Fishing Vessels, 1869 et seq.', MSS Records, H.M. Customs and Excise, Custom House, Lerwick.

Davis, F. (1968), 'Professional Socialization as Subjective Experience', in Becker, H. S. *et al.*, *Institutions and the Person*, Aldine Publishing Co., Chicago.

Dean, L. (1970), *Competitive strategy in the Newfoundland longliner fleet*, Memorial University, St. John's, Newfoundland (Unpublished Ms).

Dean, L. (1971), *The Bar-seine Fishery in Newfoundland*, Memorial University, St. John's, Newfoundland (Unpublished Ms).

Demarchi, F. (1970), 'L'Associazionismo in Provincia di Gorizia', *Forni*, Bologna.

Demarchi, F. (1967), *Societa e Spazio*, Istituto Superiore di Scienzi Sociali, Trento.

Dennis, N., Henriques, F. M., and Slaughter, C. (1957), *Coal is Our Life*, Eyre and Spottiswoode, London.

Digby, M. (1961), *La Cooperacion entre Pescadores*, Holanda.

Duncan, P., 'Conflict and Co-operation Among Trawlermen', *British Journal of Industrial Relations*, Vol. 1, No. 3, 1963, pp. 331–47.

Durkheim, E. (1947), *Division of Labour in Society*, Free Press, Glencoe, Ill.

Dynes, R. R. (1970), *Organized Behaviour in Disaster*, Heath Lexington Books, London.

Earls, J. H. (1969), 'Human Adjustment to an Exotic Environment: The Nuclear Submarine', *Archives of General Psychiatry*, Vol. 20.

Edmondston, A. (1809), *A View of the Ancient and Present State of the Zetland Islands*, Vol. 1, Edinburgh.

Faris, J. (1966), *Cat Harbour: A Newfoundland Fishing Settlement*, Memorial University Press, St. John's, Newfoundland.

Firestone, M. (1967), *Brothers and Rivals: Patrilocality in Savage Cove*, Memorial University, St. John's, Newfoundland.

Fishery Board for Scotland (1905), Annual Report, HMSO, Edinburgh.

Food and Agriculture Organization (1968), *La Situation de la Peche dans le Monde*, Rome.

Foot, P. (1967), 'The Seamen's Struggle', in R. Blackburn and C. Cockburn (eds.), *The Incompatibles*, Penguin, Harmondsworth.

Forman, S. (1967), 'Cognition and the Catch: The Location of Fishing Spots in a Coastal Brazilian Village', *Ethnology*, Vol. 6, No. 4; pp. 417–26.

Fortuna, P. (1961), 'Una Notte in Mare con i pescatori di Marano', *Julia Gens*.

Foulser, G. (1961), *Seaman's Voice*, McGibbon and Kee, London.

Frankenberg, R. (1966), *Communities in Britain*, Penguin Books, Harmondsworth.

Fraser, T. M. (1960), *Rusembilan*, Cornell University Press, Ithaca, N.Y.

Fricke, P. H. (1971), 'The Social Role of the Naval Architect', *Shipping World and Shipbuilder*, pp. 541–7.

Fricke, P. H. (1972), 'The Social Structure of the Crews of British Dry-Cargo Merchant Ships: A study of the Organization and Environment of an Occupation', University of Durham (Unpublished Ph.D. Thesis).

Friedmann, G., Naville, P. (1961), *Traite de Sociologie du Travail*, Paris.

Garano, M. (1968), 'I Pescatori di Marano', *La Cooperazione del Friuli Venezia Giulia*, No. 2.

Gerst, D. (ed.) (1968), 'De La Peche: Sur Quelques Problems Sociologiques de Professionals de la Peche Maritime, *Liaison*, No. 71.

Glaser, B. G., and Strauss, A. L. (1968), *The Discovery of Grounded Theory*, Weidenfeld and Nicolson, London.

Goffman, E. (1961), *Asylums*, Doubleday, New York.

Goodlad, C. A. (1971), *Shetland Fishing Saga*, Shetland Times Press, Lerwick.

Goodlad, A. (n.d.), *A Survey of Newfoundland Longliner Fishing* (in preparation).

Gouldner, A. W. (1955), 'Metaphysical Pathos and the Theory of Bureaucracy', *American Political Science Review*, Vol. 49.

Graham, G. (1967), 'Fisheries and Seapower', in *Historic Essays on the Atlantic Provinces*, Carelton Library, McClelland and Stewart, Toronto.

Gronseth, E., and Tiller, P. (1958), 'Father Absence in Sailor Families and its Import upon the Personality Development and Later Social Adjustment of the Children', *Nordiske Psykologi*, Monograph Series, No. 9, Oslo.

Gronseth, E. (1959), *Reactions of Seamen's Wives to Frustrations Resulting from the Absence of their Husbands*, Institute for Social Research, Oslo (Mimeo).

Halcrow, A. (1950), *The Sail Fishermen of Shetland*, Lerwick.

Harris–Jenkins, G. (1970), 'Professionals in Organization', In

Jackson, J. A., *Professions and Professionalization*, Cambridge University Press.

Hay and Co. Ltd., *MSS Records of Hay and Co. (Lerwick) Ltd.*, Lerwick.

Herbst, P. G. (1968), 'Interpersonal Distance Regulation and Affective Control on Merchant Ships', *European Journal of Social Psychology*, Vol. 1, No. 1, pp. 47–58.

Hill, J. M. M. (1972), *The Seafaring Career*, The Tavistock Institute of Human Relations, London.

Hogg, T. (1971), *Man in the Marine Environment*, UWIST, Cardiff (Unpublished seminar paper).

Hohman, E. P. (1952), *Seamen Ashore*, Yale University Press, New Haven.

Hopwood, W. H. (1971), *Preparing to be a Merchant Navy Officer: A Study in Occupational Socialization*, University of Bristol (Unpublished M.Ed. Thesis).

Horbulewicz, J. (1966), *Optymalny Czas Pobytu Zalog Rybackich Na Morzu W Swietle ich Opinni*, Morski Instytut Ryzacki, Gdynia.

Horbulewicz, J. (1968), *Charakterystyka Pracy na Trawlerach Przetworniach z Punktu Widzenia Dokuczliwosci Zagrozenia Vrazowoseia oraz Zagrozenia Zdronia Psychicznego*, Morski Instytut Rybacki, Gdynia.

Horbulewicz, J., and Filipek, B. (1969), 'Somatic Complaints and Emotional Disturbances in Fishermen Employed on Oceangoing Vessels', *Bulletin of the Institute of Marine Medicine*, Gdansk; Vol. 20, No. 1—2.

Horbulewicz, J. (1970), 'Some Agents Accompanying the increase of Disturbances in the Emotional Equilibrium of Fishermen during Deep sea Fishing', in Buczowski, Z. (ed.), *Medycyna Morska*, Wybrane Zag FTN, Gdansk.

Horbulewicz, J. (1972), 'Dissatisfaction and Departure from Employment in Maritime Professions in the Western Countries', *Technika i Gospodarka Morska*, No. 2.

Horobin, G. W. (1957), 'Community and Occupation in the Hull Fishing Industry', *British Journal of Sociology*, Vol. 8, No. 4; pp. 343–56.

Innis, H. (1954), *The Cod Fisheries* (Revised edition), University of Toronto Press.

Katz, D., and Kohn, R. L. (1966), *The Social Psychology of Organizations*, John Wiley and Sons, New York.

Kerr, M. (1958), *The People of Ship Street*, Routledge and Kegan Paul, London.

Kipling, R. (1896), *Captains Courageous*, Bantam Books, New York.

Lacour, P. (1963), 'Les Associations Volontaires dans la Peche Maritime Francaise', *Archives Internationales de Sociologie de La Co-operation*, No. 3.

Lantis, M. (1970), 'Environmental Stresses on Human Behaviour', *Archives of Environmental Health*, Vol. 17.

Lawrence, P. R., and Lorsch, J. W. (1967), *Organization and Environment*, Richard D. Irwin, Homewood, Ill.

Lazarus, R. S., Deese, J., and Hamilton, R. (1954), 'Anxiety and Stress in Learning', *Journal of Experimental Psychology*, Vol. 4y, No. 2.

Liguori, V. A. (1969), *Stability and Change in the Social Structure of Atlantic Coast Commercial Fisheries*, University (Microfilm).

Lipset, S. M., Lazarsfeld, P. F., Barton, A. M., and Linz, J. (1954), 'The Psychology of Voting. An Analysis of Political Behaviour', in Lindsey, G. (ed.), *Handbook of Social Psychology*, Cambridge University Press, Cambridge.

Lofgren, O. (1972), 'Resource management and family firms: the Swedish Fishermen', in Anderson, R. and Wadel, C. (eds.): op. cit.

Low, Rev. G. (1879), *A Tour through the Islands of Orkney and Schetland in 1774*, Edinburgh.

Lupton, T. (1963), *On the Shop Floor*, Oxford University Press.

MacIver, R. M. (1924), *Community*, London; Macmillan and Co.

Maier, N. R. F. (1952), *Principles of Human Relations*, John Wiley and Sons, New York.

Martin, K. (1972), *Some Economic Ramifications of Territoriality and Boundary Maintenance among Fishing Peoples*, Memorial University, St. John's, Newfoundland (Unpublished Ms).

Mathews, K. (1971), *Historical Fence-building*, Paper presented to the Canadian Historical Association, Annual Meeting, June.

Maurer, J. G. (ed.) (1971), *Readings in Organization Theory—Open-System Approaches*, Random-House, New York.

Mills, D. (1971), *The Pothead Whale Fishery in Newfoundland*, Memorial University, St. John's, Newfoundland (Unpublished Ms).

Milsom, C. H. (1968), *Guide to the Merchant Navy*, Brown, Son and Ferguson, Glasgow.

Missiuro, W. (1947), *Znuzenie*, Ksiazka: Wiedza, Warsaw.

Moreby, D. H. (1969), *Personnel Management in Merchant Ships*, Pergamon Press, London.

Morrill, W. T. (1967), 'Ethnoicthyology of the Cha-Cha', *Ethnology*, Vol. 6, No. 4; pp. 405–16.

Morris, T. P. I and P. (1963), *Pentonville*, Routledge & Kegan Paul, London.

Myrdal, A., and Klein, V. (1968), V. (1968), *Women's Two Roles*, Routledge Paperback, London.

Nemec, T. (1972), 'I Fish with my Brother: the Structure and Behaviour of Agnatic based Fishing Crews in a Newfoundland Fishing Community', in Andersen, R., and Wade, C. (eds.), *North Atlantic Fishermen*, op. cit.

Olivotto, R. (1892), *Marano Lagunare: Volo attraverso i Secoli*, Cividale.

Paine, R. (1957), *Coast Lapp Society*, Tromso Museum, Tromso, Vol. 1.

Pearlman, C. A., Jr. (1970), 'Separation Reactions of Married Women', *American Journal of Psychiatry*, No. 126.

Peche Maritime (1970), *Une Enquete sur la Desaffection des Jeunes pour la Grande Peche*, Peche Maritime, Paris, No. 1111.

Phillips, M. (1965), *Small Social Groups in England*, Methuen, London.

Postman, L., and Bruner, J. S. (1948), 'Perception Under Stress', *Psychological Review*.

Prandy, K. (1965), *Professional Employees*, Faber and Faber, London.

E. S. Reid Tait Collection, 'Articles of Agreement for the Cod Fishing, 1824 and 1890', Shetland County Library, Lerwick.

Reykowski, J. (1968), *Eksperymentalna Psychologia Emocji*, Ksiazka: Wiedza, Warsaw.

Reynolds, G. S. (1960), 'The Effect of Stress upon Problem Solving', *Journal of General Psychology*, No. 2.

Richardson, S. A. (1956), 'Organizational Contrasts on British and American Ships', *Administrative Science Quarterly*, Vol. 1, pp. 168–206.

Rosengren, W. R., and Bassis, M., '*Society, Organization and Technical Education: A Cross-National Study of Merchant Marine Training* (Forthcoming).

Rowntree, B. S., and Lavers, G. R. (1951), *Poverty and the Welfare State*, London.

158 SEAFARER AND COMMUNITY

Schmidtke, H. (1965), *Die Ermudung*, Bern-Stutgart.

Report of the Scottish Departmental Committee on the North Sea Fishing Industry (1914), HMSO, London.

Scottish Record Office, *Abstract Books: MSS Records of the Fishery Board for Scotland, 1821–1875*, Scottish Record Office, Edinburgh.

Sillitoe (1971), *Britain in Figures: A Handbook of Social Statistics*, Penguin Books, Harmondsworth.

Smith, H. D. (1972), *An Historical Geography of Trade in the Shetland Islands, 1550–1914*, University of Aberdeen (Unpublished Ph.D. Thesis).

Solomon, P., *et al.* (eds.) (1961), *Sensory Deprivation*, Harvard University Press, Cambridge, Mass.

Spitz, R. A. (1945), *'Hospitalism': The Psychoanalytic Study of the Child*, Vol. 1, No 1

Stiles, G. (1972 a), 'Fishermen, Wives and Radios: Aspects of Communication in a Newfoundland Fishing Community', in Andersen, R. and Wadel, C. (eds.) op. cit.

Stiles, G. (1972 b), *Reluctant Entrepreneurs: Organizational Change and Capital Management in a Newfoundland Fishery*, ISER St. John's, Newfoundland (in preparation).

Sykes, G. M. (1964), *The Society of Captives*, Princeton University Press.

Tellia, B. (1969), 'Alcuni Modelli Occidentali della Ribellione Giovanile', *Prospettive di Efficienza*, No. 3.

Tellia, B. (1971), 'L'Associazionismo Giovanile', in Demarchi, F. *et al.* (eds.), *Gioventu 1970 nel Friuli-Venezia Giulia*, Trieste.

Templemann, W. (1966), *Marine Resources of Newfoundland*, Dept. of Fisheries, Ottawa: Queen's Printer.

Thompson, J. D. (1967), *Organizations in Action*, McGraw-Hill, New York.

Tomaszewski, W. (1963), *Introduction to Psychology*, PWN, Warsaw.

Tunstall, J. (1962), *The Fishermen*, McGibbon & Kee, London.

Weybrow, B. B. (1963), 'Psychological problems of prolonged marine submergence', in Burns, N. M. *et al.* (eds.), *Unusual Environments and Human Behaviour*, Free Press, Glencoe, Ill.

Williamson, K. (1947), *The Atlantic Islands*, Memorial University Press, St. John's, Newfoundland.

Wolfgang, M. E., Savitz, L., and Johnston, N. (eds.) (1962), *The Sociology of Punishment and Correction*, John Wiley and Sons, New York.

Yates, A. J. (1965), *Frustration and Conflict*, D. Van Nostrand, Princeton.

Young, M., and Willmott, P. (1957), *Family and Kinship in East London*, Routledge & Kegan Paul, London.

Index